Microsoft 365 Copilot Prompts

AI Tools for Enhanced Productivity

Savannah Johnson

Microsoft 365 Copilot Prompts

AI Tools for Enhanced Productivity

Published by
Savannah Johnson

ISBN
9798340092847

Copyright Notice

The content of this book is protected by copyright law. It is intended for personal use only. Unauthorized reproduction, distribution, modification, sale, use, quoting, or paraphrasing of any part or all of the content of this book without the author's or publisher's consent is prohibited.

All rights for translation, adaptation, and reproduction by any means are reserved worldwide. According to the Copyright Act, any copying or reproduction strictly for private use and not for collective use is permitted. However, any total or partial representation or reproduction without the author's or rights holder's consent is illegal and constitutes copyright infringement, subject to legal penalties.

Disclaimer:

By reading this document, the reader agrees that the author is not liable for any direct or indirect losses resulting from the use of the information contained in this document, including but not limited to errors, omissions, or inaccuracies.

Copyright © Savannah Johnson – All rights reserved

TABLE OF CONTENTS

Introduction 5
   The Modern Work Crisis 10
      Diagnosing the Overwhelm of "Digital Debt" 10
      The False Promise of "Working Harder" 15
   The Co-Pilot Revolution 23
      Introducing the Prompting System as Your New OS 23
      Mapping Your Journey to AI-Powered Productivity 29

1. Build Your AI Foundation 38
   1.1 The Co-Pilot Mindset 44
      1.1.1 Moving from User to Power User 44
      1.1.2 Adopting the Augmentation Philosophy 51
   1.2 The Core Prompting Framework 59
      1.2.1 Constructing Prompts with Persona, Task, Context, and Format (PTCF) 59
      1.2.2 The Art of Iteration: Refining Prompts for Precision .. 67

2. Automate Your Communications 76
   2.1 The Zero-Inbox System 82
      2.1.1 Summarizing Long Email Threads Instantly 82
      2.1.2 Drafting High-Impact Replies in Seconds 91
   2.2 The Instant Document Drafter 102
      2.2.1 Generating First Drafts of Reports and Memos .. 102
      2.2.2 Rewriting and Refining Tone for Any Audience ... 110

3. Master Your Meetings and Collaboration 120
   3.1 The Automated Meeting Assistant 126
      3.1.1 Generating Pre-Meeting Briefings and Agendas 126
      3.1.2 Capturing Action Items and Decisions from Transcripts 135
   3.2 The Presentation Power-Up 145
      3.2.1 Creating Presentation Outlines from Documents 145
      3.2.2 Generating Speaker Notes and Key Talking Points ..

4. Amplify Your Analytical Power..164

   4.1 The Data Interrogation Engine......................................170

      4.1.1 Generating Formulas from Natural Language Descriptions... 170

      4.1.2 Identifying Key Trends and Outliers in Datasets. 179

   4.2 The Strategic Insights Generator.................................. 189

      4.2.1 Creating SWOT Analyses from Business Documents... 189

      4.2.2 Summarizing Complex Research for Executive Briefings.. 197

5. Integrate Your AI Co-Pilot.. 207

   5.1 The End-to-End Workflow Automator.......................... 213

      5.1.1 The Project Kick-Off: From Initial Idea to Action Plan..213

      5.1.2 The Monthly Report: From Raw Data to Final Presentation..222

   5.2 The Personalized Productivity System........................ 230

      5.2.1 Customizing Prompts for Your Specific Role and Industry.. 230

      5.2.2 Building a Personal Library of High-Performance Prompts..239

Conclusion.. 247

Acknowledgements..256

Introduction

Every morning at 7:30 AM, I watch the same scene unfold across office buildings worldwide. Professionals like you settle into their desks, open their laptops, and immediately feel the familiar weight of digital overwhelm pressing down on their shoulders. The inbox shows 47 unread messages from overnight. Three meeting invitations demand immediate responses. A project deadline looms, but the required data lives scattered across seventeen different email threads, six shared documents, and countless chat conversations.

I know this feeling intimately because I lived it for years. As a project manager early in my career, I would arrive at work energized and ready to tackle strategic challenges, only to find myself drowning in administrative quicksand before 9 AM. By lunch, I had sent dozens of emails, attended two "quick sync" meetings that solved nothing, and spent an hour hunting through document versions to find the latest project specifications. The work that truly mattered, the strategic thinking that could drive real impact, got pushed to evening hours when my brain was already fried.

This is the modern work crisis, and if you recognize yourself in this description, you are not alone. Across every industry and organization size, professionals are experiencing what I call "digital debt." Like financial debt, digital debt compounds daily. Each unprocessed email creates follow-up emails. Every inefficient meeting spawns three more meetings to clarify what should have been decided in the first place. Every document created without clear structure becomes a source of confusion that generates hours of additional clarification work.

The numbers paint a stark picture. Knowledge workers now spend over 60% of their time on "work about work" rather than the actual strategic, creative, and analytical tasks that drive business value. We check email every six minutes. We attend an average of 23 hours of meetings per week, with 67% of senior managers reporting they spend too much time in meetings to complete their own work. The tools that promised to make us more productive have instead created an avalanche of low-value busy work that buries our highest-impact activities.

Here's what frustrates me most: when faced with this overwhelm, most professionals reach for the wrong solutions. They work longer hours, trying to power through the digital debt with brute force. They attend time management seminars that teach them to organize their chaos more efficiently rather than eliminate it. They adopt new productivity apps that promise to be the "one tool to rule them all," only to discover these tools create their own maintenance overhead.

Working harder is not the answer. Working more hours is not the answer. Adding more tools is definitely not the answer. The industrial age taught us that productivity came from optimizing human effort, but we are no longer living in the industrial age. We are living in the intelligence age, where the professionals who thrive are those who learn to amplify their cognitive capacity through artificial intelligence.

This brings us to the pivotal moment we find ourselves in today. Microsoft 365 Copilot, along with similar AI tools, represents the most significant productivity breakthrough since the personal computer. For the first time in business history, every professional has access to an AI assistant capable of drafting emails, summarizing documents, analyzing data, creating presentations, and generating insights from complex information sets. The technology exists right now, integrated into the tools you already use every day, to eliminate the majority of your digital debt.

Yet here's the challenge: most professionals approach AI tools like tourists in a foreign country, pointing at menu items and hoping for the best. They ask Copilot simple questions like "summarize this email" and wonder why the results feel generic and unhelpful. They treat AI like a search engine rather than the sophisticated reasoning partner it actually is. This casual approach produces casual results, leaving them disappointed and skeptical about AI's true potential.

The difference between casual AI users and power users comes down to one critical skill: strategic prompt engineering. While others are asking basic questions, power users are crafting precise instructions that transform AI from a novelty into an indispensable productivity engine. They understand that AI is not about finding information; it's about generating customized solutions for their specific professional challenges.

Strategic prompt engineering is the new literacy of the modern workplace. Just as computer literacy was essential in the 1990s and internet literacy was essential in the 2000s, prompt engineering literacy will determine who thrives in the AI-powered workplace of the 2020s and beyond. This skill allows you to delegate not just simple tasks, but complex cognitive work to your AI assistant, freeing you to focus on the strategic thinking, creative problem-solving, and relationship building that only humans can provide.

Throughout my work with Fortune 500 companies and high-performing professionals across North America and Europe, I have developed a proprietary system for maximizing Microsoft 365 Copilot's productivity impact. This system, which I call the PTCF Framework (Persona, Task, Context, Format), transforms how professionals interact with AI by providing a structured methodology for crafting prompts that consistently deliver exceptional results.

The PTCF Framework is built on a simple but powerful principle: AI assistants, like human assistants, perform best when given clear, specific instructions that include context about your role, your objective, the relevant background information, and the desired outcome format. Instead of asking "summarize this email," a power user employing the PTCF Framework might instruct Copilot to "Act as a project manager reviewing client communications. Analyze this email thread between our team and the client, identify the three most critical decisions that were made, and format your response as a bulleted list with each decision followed by its business impact."

This book will teach you to think like a director of AI rather than a consumer of AI. You will learn to see Microsoft 365 Copilot not as a fancy autocomplete feature, but as your personal chief of staff, capable of handling the administrative and analytical heavy lifting that currently consumes your most productive hours. By the end of our journey together, you will have a complete system for reclaiming your time and amplifying your professional impact.

Here's the roadmap for your transformation. We will begin by building your AI foundation, establishing the mindset and core framework that underlies all advanced Copilot usage. Next, we will automate your communications, teaching you to handle email and document creation with unprecedented speed and quality. From there, we will master meetings and collaboration, turning your most time-consuming professional activities into efficient, AI-assisted workflows. We will then amplify your analytical power, showing you how to extract insights from data and documents that would take human analysts hours to uncover. Finally, we will integrate everything into a personalized productivity system that adapts to your specific role and industry.

This is not a book about technology. This is a book about reclaiming your professional life. By mastering strategic prompt engineering, you will move from reactive task execution to proactive strategic leadership. You will delegate your busy work to AI and reclaim your time for the work that truly matters: the creative thinking, strategic planning, and relationship building that drives real business value and career advancement.

Your journey to AI-powered productivity begins now.

The Modern Work Crisis

Diagnosing the Overwhelm of "Digital Debt"

Digital debt operates like financial debt, compounding silently in the background until it becomes impossible to ignore. I have observed this phenomenon across hundreds of professionals in my consulting practice, and I can tell you with certainty that most people underestimate the true scope of their digital burden. Unlike financial debt, which shows up clearly on statements and credit reports, digital debt hides in your workflows, masquerading as "just part of the job."

Let me guide you through a comprehensive diagnostic process to reveal the true extent of your digital debt. This systematic assessment will help you understand exactly how much of your cognitive capacity is being consumed by administrative overhead rather than strategic work.

The Digital Debt Assessment Framework

Use this structured evaluation to quantify your current digital debt load. I recommend completing this assessment honestly, as the results will form the foundation for everything we build together in this book.

Step 1: Email Debt Analysis

Begin by examining your email patterns over the past week. Open your email client and gather these specific data points:

- **Current inbox count:** Record the total number of unread emails in your primary inbox right now
- **Daily email volume:** Count how many emails you received yesterday (check your sent folder for replies to estimate incoming volume)
- **Response time lag:** Identify your three most recent important emails and calculate how many hours elapsed

between receiving them and sending a meaningful response
- **Thread complexity:** Find your longest email thread from the past month and count how many back-and-forth exchanges occurred before reaching resolution

Email Debt Severity Indicators:

- **Mild Digital Debt:** 10-50 unread emails, same-day responses to priority items
- **Moderate Digital Debt:** 51-200 unread emails, 24-48 hour response delays
- **Severe Digital Debt:** 200+ unread emails, responses delayed by multiple days or forgotten entirely

Step 2: Meeting Overhead Calculation

Document your meeting reality using these measurement criteria:

- **Weekly meeting hours:** Add up all scheduled meetings from your calendar last week, including "quick calls" and informal check-ins
- **Preparation time multiplier:** For each meeting, estimate how many minutes you spent preparing (reviewing agendas, gathering materials, catching up on context)
- **Follow-up task generation:** Count how many action items or follow-up emails resulted from your meetings last week
- **Meeting effectiveness ratio:** Calculate what percentage of your meeting time was spent on decisions versus discussion, updates, or clarification

Meeting Debt Warning Signs:

- Spending more than 20 hours per week in meetings
- Preparation time exceeding 25% of actual meeting duration
- More than three follow-up tasks generated per meeting
- Less than 30% of meeting time devoted to actual decision-making

Step 3: Document and File Management Debt

Evaluate your information organization system through these specific checkpoints:

- **File retrieval time:** Time yourself finding a document you worked on two weeks ago. Record how many locations you searched and how long it took
- **Version confusion incidents:** Count how many times in the past month you worked on an outdated document version or had to clarify "which version is current"
- **Document recreation frequency:** Identify instances where you recreated information that already existed somewhere in your systems
- **Knowledge transfer bottlenecks:** List how many times colleagues asked you to locate or explain information that should be systematically accessible

Step 4: Communication Channel Fragmentation Assessment

Map your communication ecosystem and identify redundancy patterns:

- **Active communication platforms:** List every platform where you receive work-related messages (email, Teams, Slack, WhatsApp, text, phone calls)
- **Message scatter analysis:** Choose one recent project and count how many different platforms contained relevant communications about it
- **Context switching frequency:** Estimate how many times per day you switch between communication platforms to maintain full awareness
- **Missed message incidents:** Recall instances from the past month where important information was missed because it arrived through an unexpected channel

Step 5: Cognitive Load Impact Measurement

Assess how digital debt affects your strategic capacity:

- **Deep work availability:** Calculate your longest uninterrupted work session last week without checking email, messages, or responding to notifications
- **Task completion satisfaction:** Rate your satisfaction level (1-10) with the quality of work you produced during your most complex project last week
- **Mental energy depletion:** Identify the time of day when you typically feel mentally drained and compare it to your administrative task completion patterns
- **Strategic thinking time:** Estimate how many hours you spent last week on forward-thinking, creative, or strategic activities versus reactive administrative work

The Digital Debt Diagnosis Results

Once you complete this assessment, you will likely recognize patterns that have been invisible to you before. Most professionals I work with discover that their digital debt consumes 60-70% of their available cognitive capacity, leaving only a fraction of their mental energy for the work that truly drives business value and career advancement.

Critical Digital Debt Symptoms

Watch for these common manifestations that indicate your digital debt has reached critical levels:

- **The Sunday Night Dread:** Feeling anxious about Monday morning because you know your inbox will be overwhelming
- **The Endless Catch-Up Cycle:** Spending the first two hours of each day processing overnight communications instead of tackling priority projects
- **The Context Loss Problem:** Regularly needing to re-read email threads or meeting notes to remember previous decisions

- **The Reactive Work Trap:** Finding that your most productive work happens after normal business hours when communications stop
- **The Decision Delay Pattern:** Postponing important decisions because gathering the relevant information feels too overwhelming

The Compounding Effect

Digital debt compounds in ways that most professionals do not anticipate. Each unprocessed email creates the potential for follow-up emails. Every inefficient meeting spawns additional meetings to clarify what should have been decided. Each document created without proper organization becomes a future time sink when someone needs to locate or update that information.

I recently worked with a marketing director at a global technology company who calculated that his team spent 14 hours per week just locating and organizing information that already existed within their systems. That represents 35% of their collective work time devoted to administrative archaeology rather than campaign development or strategic planning.

The Hidden Cost of Digital Debt

The true cost of digital debt extends far beyond time management. When your cognitive capacity is consumed by administrative overhead, you lose access to your highest-value professional capabilities. Strategic thinking requires sustained attention and mental clarity. Creative problem-solving demands the ability to hold multiple concepts simultaneously while exploring novel connections. Leadership presence requires being fully present and responsive to nuanced human dynamics.

Digital debt fragments your attention, depletes your mental energy, and reduces your professional impact to a series of reactive responses rather than proactive strategic contributions. This is why traditional productivity advice fails. Organizing your existing chaos more efficiently still leaves you buried in chaos, just with better labels.

The Breaking Point Recognition

The professionals who achieve breakthrough productivity results share one common experience: they reach a breaking point where the current system becomes obviously unsustainable. This diagnostic process is designed to help you reach that recognition before digital debt completely overwhelms your capacity for strategic work.

Your digital debt is not a character flaw or a time management failure. It is the predictable result of applying industrial age productivity strategies to information age challenges. The solution requires a fundamental shift in how you approach administrative work, and that shift begins with recognizing that your current approach cannot scale to meet modern professional demands.

The assessment you just completed reveals the scope of the problem we will solve together. In the next section, we will examine why the conventional solution of "working harder" only makes digital debt worse, setting the stage for the revolutionary approach that will transform your professional effectiveness.

THE FALSE PROMISE OF "WORKING HARDER"

The greatest lie told in modern professional culture is that productivity problems can be solved by working harder, longer, or with more intensity. I have watched countless intelligent professionals fall into this trap, believing that if they just pushed themselves a little more, stayed a little later, or checked email a little more frequently, they would finally get ahead of their workload.

This conventional wisdom is not just wrong. It is actively destructive, creating a vicious cycle that generates more work while delivering diminishing returns on your time and energy investment.

The Hard Work Trap: A Systematic Analysis

Let me show you exactly why the "work harder" approach fails by breaking down its fundamental flaws through a structured analysis of what actually happens when professionals attempt to solve digital debt through increased effort.

Problem 1: The Volume Multiplication Effect

When you respond to increased workload by working longer hours, you inadvertently signal to your organization and colleagues that you have unlimited capacity. This creates a feedback loop:

- **Initial Response:** You stay late to clear your inbox and catch up on projects
- **Organizational Signal:** Your availability increases, making you the go-to person for additional requests
- **Volume Increase:** More work flows to you because you have proven you can handle it
- **Escalation Pattern:** The new baseline becomes your extended hours, with additional work piling on top

Problem 2: The Quality Degradation Cycle

Extended work sessions produce measurably worse outcomes, not better ones. Cognitive research demonstrates that decision-making quality deteriorates predictably with fatigue:

- **Hours 1-6:** Optimal cognitive performance and decision quality
- **Hours 7-10:** 15-25% reduction in critical thinking capacity
- **Hours 11+:** Up to 50% degradation in complex problem-solving ability

- **Cumulative Effect:** Poor decisions made during extended hours create additional work the next day

Problem 3: The Administrative Expansion Phenomenon

Working harder typically means spending more time on low-value administrative tasks, not strategic work. I have observed this pattern across hundreds of professionals:

- **Email Response Acceleration:** Faster email responses train others to expect immediate replies, increasing overall email volume
- **Meeting Availability Increase:** Longer work days mean more meeting slots, leading to more meetings being scheduled
- **Documentation Overhead Growth:** Extended hours get filled with process-oriented work rather than outcome-oriented work
- **Context Switching Multiplication:** Longer days create more opportunities for interruptions and task fragmentation

Case Study: The Project Manager's Productivity Paradox

I once worked with a project manager at a multinational consulting firm who epitomized the "work harder" approach. When I first met Marcus, he was working 12-hour days and felt constantly behind. He believed his solution was to extend to 14-hour days.

Here is what actually happened during his attempted productivity increase:

Week 1-2: Initial Effort Expansion

- **Time Investment:** Increased daily work from 10 hours to 14 hours
- **Inbox Processing:** Responded to emails within 30 minutes instead of 2 hours

- **Meeting Availability:** Accepted all meeting invitations to appear collaborative
- **Project Oversight:** Personally reviewed every deliverable to ensure quality

Week 3-4: Unintended Consequences

- **Email Volume:** Increased by 40% because fast responses encouraged more frequent communication
- **Meeting Load:** Grew from 15 hours per week to 25 hours per week due to increased availability
- **Quality Issues:** Three projects required rework because fatigue led to oversight errors
- **Team Dependency:** Team members began escalating routine decisions because Marcus was always available

Week 5-6: System Breakdown

- **Burnout Symptoms:** Physical exhaustion, decision fatigue, and irritability appeared
- **Strategic Thinking:** Zero time allocated to planning, process improvement, or strategic initiatives
- **Career Impact:** Missed a promotion opportunity because he was too busy executing to demonstrate leadership vision
- **Personal Cost:** Family relationships strained, health declined, job satisfaction plummeted

The Root Cause Analysis

The fundamental problem with working harder is that it addresses symptoms rather than causes. Digital debt is a systems problem that requires a systems solution, not a personal effort solution.

Systems Problem Indicators:

- **Input Control:** You cannot control the volume of requests entering your workflow

- **Processing Efficiency:** Current methods for handling information are inefficient
- **Output Quality:** Existing approaches produce inconsistent results that require rework
- **Scalability Limits:** Human cognitive capacity has finite limits that cannot be exceeded through willpower

Why Traditional Time Management Fails

Most productivity advice assumes that better organization of existing processes will solve workload problems. This approach fails because it optimizes inefficient systems rather than replacing them.

Traditional Advice Limitations:

1. **Priority Matrix Methods**
    - **Theory:** Categorize tasks by urgency and importance
    - **Reality:** 80% of professional work feels both urgent and important
    - **Failure Point:** Does not reduce total workload or improve processing efficiency
2. **Time Blocking Strategies**
    - **Theory:** Schedule specific time slots for different types of work
    - **Reality:** Knowledge work is unpredictable and interruption-heavy
    - **Failure Point:** Blocks get disrupted, creating planning overhead without productivity gains
3. **Inbox Zero Techniques**
    - **Theory:** Process emails using decision rules (delete, delegate, defer, do)
    - **Reality:** Email volume exceeds processing capacity regardless of method

- **Failure Point:** Organizes existing chaos without reducing the chaos generation rate

The Energy Depletion Factor

Working harder depletes your most valuable professional resource: cognitive energy. Unlike physical energy, cognitive energy cannot be restored through caffeine or short breaks. It requires genuine recovery time that the "work harder" approach eliminates.

Cognitive Energy Depletion Stages:

1. **Peak Performance:** Creative thinking, strategic planning, complex problem-solving
2. **Competent Execution:** Routine task completion, standard decision-making
3. **Administrative Mode:** Email processing, meeting attendance, simple responses
4. **Survival Mode:** Reactive responses, minimal quality standards, error-prone work

Most professionals spending 12+ hours per day working operate primarily in stages 3 and 4, which explains why increased effort yields decreased results.

The Opportunity Cost Reality

Every hour spent working harder is an hour not spent working smarter. While you are processing your 200th email of the day, you are not:

- **Developing Systems:** Creating processes that prevent problems rather than solving them
- **Learning Tools:** Mastering technologies that could automate routine work
- **Strategic Planning:** Thinking ahead to prevent future workload crises

- **Skill Development:** Building capabilities that increase your professional value
- **Relationship Building:** Investing in connections that create long-term career opportunities

The Breaking Point Recognition

The professionals who achieve breakthrough productivity results share one common experience: they recognize that working harder is a dead-end strategy. This recognition typically occurs when:

- **Physical Limits:** Health problems force acknowledgment that the pace is unsustainable
- **Performance Decline:** Work quality deteriorates despite increased effort
- **Opportunity Loss:** Important career or personal opportunities are missed due to overcommitment
- **System Breakdown:** The existing approach fails completely during a high-stakes situation

The Paradigm Shift Requirement

Moving beyond the "work harder" trap requires a fundamental shift in how you think about productivity. Instead of asking "How can I do more?" you must start asking "How can I accomplish the same results with less effort?"

This shift requires accepting three uncomfortable truths:

1. **Your current approach is the problem, not the solution**
2. **Working harder will make your situation worse, not better**
3. **Breakthrough results require breakthrough methods, not incremental improvements**

The solution is not about managing your time better or organizing your tasks more efficiently. The solution is about fundamentally changing how work gets done by leveraging artificial intelligence to handle the cognitive overhead that currently consumes your professional capacity.

In the next section, we will explore how AI tools like Microsoft 365 Copilot represent a completely different approach to professional productivity, one that allows you to delegate routine cognitive work and reclaim your mental energy for the strategic thinking that drives real business value and career advancement.

The Co-Pilot Revolution

Introducing the Prompting System as Your New OS

The solution to your productivity crisis does not lie in working harder, adopting more apps, or attending another time management seminar. The solution lies in mastering a single, systematic approach to communicating with artificial intelligence. I call this approach the **PTCF Framework: Persona, Task, Context, Format**, and it will become your new operating system for professional productivity.

The Chief of Staff Analogy: Understanding AI Communication

Before diving into the framework itself, you must understand how to think about Microsoft 365 Copilot. Stop thinking of it as a search engine or a fancy autocomplete feature. Instead, think of Copilot as your personal chief of staff, an incredibly capable assistant who can handle complex cognitive work but needs precise instructions to deliver exceptional results.

Consider how a senior executive works with their chief of staff:

- **Clear Role Definition:** The chief of staff understands their position and responsibilities within the organization
- **Specific Task Assignment:** The executive provides detailed instructions about what needs to be accomplished
- **Relevant Context:** The chief of staff receives background information necessary to complete the task effectively
- **Expected Output Format:** The executive specifies exactly how they want the results presented

This same communication structure applies to working with AI. The executives who get the most value from their chiefs of staff are those who provide clear, comprehensive instructions. The same principle governs AI productivity: structured prompts produce superior results.

The PTCF Framework: Your Systematic Approach to AI Communication

The PTCF Framework transforms chaotic AI interactions into predictable, high-quality outcomes. Each letter represents a critical component that must be included in every professional prompt you create.

P - Persona: Defining the AI's Professional Role

The Persona component establishes the AI's professional identity and expertise for the specific task. This is not optional fluff; it fundamentally changes how the AI processes information and generates responses.

Core Persona Elements:

- **Professional Title:** Specify the exact role (e.g., "Act as a project manager," "Act as a financial analyst")
- **Industry Context:** Include relevant industry when applicable (e.g., "Act as a marketing manager in the technology sector")
- **Expertise Level:** Define the sophistication level (e.g., "Act as a senior consultant," "Act as an executive assistant")

Why Persona Matters:

- **Response Structure:** Different professional roles organize information differently
- **Language Style:** A CFO communicates differently than a project coordinator
- **Priority Focus:** Each role emphasizes different aspects of the same information
- **Decision Framework:** Professional roles apply different criteria for evaluation and recommendation

T - Task: Specifying the Exact Objective

The Task component defines precisely what you want the AI to accomplish. Vague tasks produce vague results. Specific tasks produce actionable outcomes.

Task Specification Requirements:

- **Action Verb:** Start with a clear, specific verb (analyze, summarize, create, draft, compare)
- **Scope Definition:** Specify exactly what should be included or excluded
- **Success Criteria:** Define what constitutes a successful completion
- **Constraints:** Include any limitations or requirements

Task Examples:

- **Vague:** "Help me with this email"
- **Specific:** "Draft a professional follow-up email requesting the quarterly sales report that was due yesterday"
- **Vague:** "Look at this data"
- **Specific:** "Analyze this monthly revenue data and identify the top 3 performing product categories with percentage growth rates"

C - Context: Providing Essential Background Information

The Context component supplies the AI with relevant background information necessary to complete the task effectively. Context determines the quality and relevance of the output.

Context Categories:

- **Situational Background:** Current circumstances affecting the task
- **Stakeholder Information:** Who will receive or use the output
- **Historical Context:** Relevant past events or decisions

- **Organizational Context:** Company culture, industry norms, or specific requirements
- **Deadline Information:** Urgency level and time constraints

Context Implementation:

- **Include:** Information that directly affects how the task should be completed
- **Exclude:** Irrelevant details that might confuse or distract the AI
- **Prioritize:** Lead with the most important contextual information

F - Format: Defining the Output Structure

The Format component specifies exactly how you want the results presented. This ensures the output is immediately usable without additional processing.

Format Specification Options:

- **Document Type:** Email, memo, report, presentation outline, bullet points
- **Structure Requirements:** Numbered lists, headings, tables, paragraphs
- **Length Specifications:** Word count, number of points, page limits
- **Style Guidelines:** Formal, casual, technical, executive summary
- **Audience Considerations:** Internal team, external client, senior leadership

The PTCF Framework in Action: A Complete Example

Here is how the PTCF Framework transforms a typical productivity request from mediocre to exceptional:

Before PTCF (Typical Approach): "Summarize this email thread"

After PTCF (Systematic Approach):

Persona: "Act as an experienced project manager"

Task: "Analyze this email thread between our development team and the client, then create a comprehensive summary that identifies all key decisions, outstanding issues, and required actions"

Context: "This is a high-priority client project with a deadline next Friday. The client has been concerned about timeline delays, and our executive team needs to understand the current status for tomorrow's steering committee meeting"

Format: "Present your analysis in three sections: (1) Key Decisions Made (bulleted list), (2) Outstanding Issues (table with issue, owner, deadline), (3) Immediate Actions Required (numbered list with priority levels)"

The Systematic Advantage: Why Structure Beats Randomness

Random prompting produces random results. The PTCF Framework produces consistent, professional-quality outcomes because it addresses how AI systems actually process and generate information.

Technical Reasoning Behind the Framework:

1. **Consistency:** The same prompt structure will produce similar quality results across different scenarios
2. **Scalability:** You can apply this framework to any professional task across any Microsoft 365 application
3. **Training Effect:** Regular use of structured prompts improves your ability to identify and communicate requirements
4. **Quality Control:** The framework forces you to think through exactly what you need before making the request

Implementation Strategy: Making PTCF Your Default Approach

Converting to the PTCF Framework requires systematic adoption, not casual experimentation. Here is your implementation pathway:

Phase 1: Recognition (Week 1)

- Identify your five most frequent AI requests (email summarization, document drafting, data analysis, meeting preparation, report creation)
- Document your current prompting approach for each scenario
- Note the inconsistent quality of your current results

Phase 2: Conversion (Week 2-3)

- Rewrite your frequent requests using the PTCF Framework
- Test each converted prompt and compare results to your previous approach
- Save your successful PTCF prompts for reuse

Phase 3: Expansion (Week 4+)

- Apply PTCF to new professional scenarios as they arise
- Refine your persona definitions based on output quality
- Build a personal library of high-performance prompts

The Operating System Mentality

The PTCF Framework is not just a prompting method; it is your new operating system for professional productivity. Just as Windows or macOS provides the foundational structure for all computer operations, PTCF provides the foundational structure for all AI interactions.

Operating System Characteristics:

- **Universal Application:** Works across all Microsoft 365 Copilot applications
- **Consistent Interface:** Same structure regardless of the specific task

- **Scalable Performance:** Handles simple requests and complex workflows equally well
- **Continuous Improvement:** Gets more effective as you become more skilled at implementation

The Competitive Advantage Reality

Professionals who master structured prompting will gain an insurmountable productivity advantage over those who continue with random, unstructured AI interactions. This advantage compounds over time as structured users build libraries of proven prompts while random users continue to struggle with inconsistent results.

The PTCF Framework is your pathway to joining the ranks of AI power users who have transformed their professional effectiveness. In the next section, I will show you exactly how this transformation unfolds and what your journey to AI-powered productivity will look like.

Mapping Your Journey to AI-Powered Productivity

Your transformation from overwhelmed professional to AI-powered productivity master follows a deliberate, systematic pathway. I have designed this journey to build your capabilities progressively, ensuring each stage prepares you for the next level of mastery. By the end of this book, you will have evolved from someone who reacts to digital chaos into someone who proactively delegates routine work to AI, freeing your mental capacity for strategic thinking and high-impact activities.

Your Transformation Promise: From Reactive to Strategic

Here is the specific transformation you will achieve by mastering the PTCF Framework across Microsoft 365 Copilot:

Current State (Before):

- Spending 60-70% of your time on administrative tasks and low-value work
- Reacting to emails, meetings, and requests as they arrive
- Struggling to find time for strategic thinking and creative problem-solving
- Feeling constantly behind despite working longer hours
- Using AI tools randomly with inconsistent, frustrating results

Future State (After):

- Delegating 80% of routine cognitive work to your AI co-pilot
- Proactively managing your workflow with systematic AI assistance
- Allocating 60% of your time to strategic, creative, and relationship-building activities
- Completing administrative work in a fraction of the current time
- Operating as an AI power user with predictable, professional-quality results

The Five-Stage Mastery Journey

Your progression follows a carefully structured learning path that builds essential capabilities in the optimal sequence:

Stage 1: Build Your AI Foundation

Learning Objective: Establish the mindset and technical framework that underlies all advanced AI productivity work.

What You Will Master:

1. **The Co-Pilot Mindset Transformation**
    - Shift from thinking like an AI "user" to thinking like an AI "director"

- Adopt the augmentation philosophy that preserves human strategic value
- Understand how to delegate cognitive work while maintaining control

2. **The PTCF Framework Implementation**

    - Learn to construct every prompt with Persona, Task, Context, and Format components
    - Practice the systematic approach that eliminates random, inconsistent results
    - Master the iterative refinement process for optimizing prompt performance

Key Outcome: You will possess the foundational knowledge and structured approach needed to achieve professional-quality results from any AI interaction.

Stage 2: Automate Your Communications

Learning Objective: Apply the PTCF Framework to eliminate the two biggest time sinks in modern professional work: email management and document creation.

What You Will Master:

1. **The Zero-Inbox System**

    - Summarize complex email threads instantly with precision prompts
    - Draft professional replies in seconds using structured templates
    - Process your inbox 5x faster while improving response quality

2. **The Instant Document Drafter**

    - Generate first drafts of reports, memos, and proposals on command

- Rewrite and refine content for different audiences automatically
- Defeat blank page syndrome and reduce document creation time by 70%

Specific Skills You Will Gain:

- Copy-pasteable prompts for the 15 most common email scenarios
- Templates for generating business documents across 10 professional contexts
- Techniques for adapting tone and style for any audience level

Key Outcome: Email and document work that previously consumed 20+ hours per week will require fewer than 5 hours while producing higher quality results.

Stage 3: Master Your Meetings and Collaboration

Learning Objective: Transform meetings from time-wasting obligations into efficient, AI-enhanced strategic sessions.

What You Will Master:

1. **The Automated Meeting Assistant**
   - Generate comprehensive pre-meeting briefings from chat histories and documents
   - Extract actionable decisions and follow-up items from meeting transcripts
   - Walk into every meeting fully prepared with AI-generated insights
2. **The Presentation Power-Up**
   - Create presentation outlines from existing documents in minutes
   - Generate compelling speaker notes and talking points automatically

- Develop professional presentations 80% faster than traditional methods

Specific Skills You Will Gain:

- Pre-meeting preparation workflows that transform you into the most informed participant
- Post-meeting follow-up systems that ensure nothing falls through the cracks
- Presentation creation processes that eliminate hours of formatting and content development

Key Outcome: Meeting preparation time drops from hours to minutes, while your perceived competence and leadership presence increase dramatically.

Stage 4: Amplify Your Analytical Power

Learning Objective: Become a data-driven strategist by leveraging AI to uncover insights and generate strategic recommendations.

What You Will Master:

1. **The Data Interrogation Engine**
    - Generate complex Excel formulas using natural language descriptions
    - Identify key trends, patterns, and outliers in datasets without technical expertise
    - Transform raw data into actionable intelligence automatically
2. **The Strategic Insights Generator**
    - Create comprehensive SWOT analyses from business documents
    - Summarize complex research into executive-level briefings
    - Generate strategic recommendations based on information synthesis

Specific Skills You Will Gain:

- Natural language formula generation that eliminates Excel complexity
- Data analysis techniques that reveal hidden business insights
- Strategic analysis capabilities that position you as a business intelligence resource

Key Outcome: You will operate as a strategic analyst regardless of your technical background, using AI to uncover insights that drive business decisions.

Stage 5: Integrate Your AI Co-Pilot

Learning Objective: Orchestrate complete, multi-application workflows that demonstrate true AI productivity mastery.

What You Will Master:

1. **The End-to-End Workflow Automator**

    - Execute complete project workflows across Word, PowerPoint, Excel, and Teams
    - Chain AI tasks seamlessly from initial concept to final deliverable
    - Demonstrate the compound power of systematic AI integration

2. **The Personalized Productivity System**

    - Customize the PTCF Framework for your specific role and industry
    - Build a personal library of high-performance prompts tuned to your recurring tasks
    - Establish continuous improvement processes for ongoing optimization

Specific Skills You Will Gain:

- Multi-app workflow orchestration that showcases advanced AI competency
- Prompt customization techniques for maximum personal relevance
- System maintenance practices that ensure long-term productivity gains

Key Outcome: You will operate as a complete AI productivity professional, capable of handling complex business challenges with AI-assisted efficiency that sets you apart from colleagues.

Your Progressive Skill Development Path

The learning journey follows this structured progression:

Weeks 1-2: Foundation Building

- Master the PTCF Framework basics
- Complete your first successful prompt engineering tasks
- Experience the quality difference between structured and random prompting

Weeks 3-4: Communication Automation

- Implement zero-inbox email management
- Begin generating documents automatically
- Achieve first major time savings in daily work

Weeks 5-6: Meeting and Collaboration Enhancement

- Transform meeting preparation and follow-up processes
- Create professional presentations in minutes
- Establish reputation as highly prepared and efficient professional

Weeks 7-8: Analytical Power Development

- Begin generating insights from data and documents

- Create strategic analyses that demonstrate business acumen
- Position yourself as data-driven decision maker

Weeks 9-10: Complete Integration

- Execute end-to-end workflows across multiple applications
- Customize and optimize your personal productivity system
- Achieve full transformation from reactive worker to strategic professional

The Commitment Required for Success

This transformation requires consistent application of the PTCF Framework rather than casual experimentation. Your success depends on:

Time Investment: 30 minutes daily for deliberate practice and prompt refinement **Systematic Application:** Using structured prompts for all AI interactions, not just occasional tasks
Progressive Building: Mastering each stage before advancing to the next level **Continuous Improvement:** Regularly updating and optimizing your prompt library

Your Competitive Advantage Timeline

The productivity advantages compound rapidly as you progress through the mastery journey:

- **Week 2:** First noticeable time savings in email and document work
- **Month 1:** 30-40% reduction in administrative task time
- **Month 2:** Colleagues begin noticing your enhanced efficiency and preparation quality
- **Month 3:** Full transformation into AI-powered strategic professional
- **Ongoing:** Continuous competitive advantage as you refine and expand capabilities

Your journey begins immediately with the first chapter, where you will build the foundational mindset and technical framework that makes everything else possible.

1. Build Your AI Foundation

You now understand the problem: digital debt has consumed your professional life, working harder only makes it worse, and random AI interactions produce frustrating, inconsistent results. You also understand the solution: the PTCF Framework provides a systematic approach to AI communication that transforms Microsoft 365 Copilot from a novelty into a productivity engine.

What you need now is the foundation that makes systematic AI productivity possible. This chapter bridges the gap between understanding the problem and implementing the solution by establishing the two essential pillars that support everything else in this book.

The Foundation Principle: Simplicity Over Complexity

Before diving into specific techniques, I need to address a critical misconception that derails most professionals' AI productivity efforts. The misconception is that AI mastery requires learning hundreds of different prompts, tricks, and techniques across dozens of scenarios.

This approach fails for the same reason that memorizing 500 Excel formulas fails: it focuses on tactics without understanding principles. The professionals who achieve breakthrough results with AI do not know more tricks; they understand the underlying system that generates consistent success across any scenario.

True AI productivity mastery rests on exactly two foundational concepts:

1. **The Co-Pilot Mindset:** How you think about your relationship with AI

2. **The Core Prompting Framework:** The systematic method for communicating with AI

These two pillars support every advanced technique you will learn in subsequent chapters. Master these foundations, and every email automation, meeting preparation, data analysis, and workflow integration becomes a straightforward application of proven principles.

Why Foundation Matters: The Skyscraper Principle

I learned this principle while consulting for a multinational construction firm. The CEO explained that skyscrapers require disproportionate foundation investment. A 50-story building does not need a foundation twice as deep as a 25-story building; it needs a foundation four times as deep. The foundation investment determines the ultimate height potential.

AI productivity follows the same principle. Professionals who skip foundation work hit a ceiling quickly. They can handle basic tasks but struggle with complex, multi-step workflows. They achieve modest time savings but never break through to strategic transformation.

Professionals who invest in foundation work scale their capabilities exponentially. They start with the same basic tasks but quickly advance to orchestrating complete business processes across multiple applications. Their AI productivity compounds rather than plateaus.

The Two-Pillar Architecture

Your AI foundation consists of two interconnected but distinct components:

Pillar 1: The Co-Pilot Mindset

The Co-Pilot Mindset addresses the psychological and strategic aspects of AI interaction. This pillar answers fundamental questions about how you position yourself in relation to AI:

- **Role Definition:** How do you maintain human strategic value while delegating cognitive work?
- **Control Balance:** How do you harness AI power without becoming dependent on AI decisions?
- **Value Positioning:** How do you use AI to enhance rather than replace your professional capabilities?
- **Growth Trajectory:** How do you evolve your skills as AI capabilities expand?

The Co-Pilot Mindset transforms you from someone who uses AI tools into someone who directs AI systems. This distinction determines whether AI makes you more productive or just busier.

Pillar 2: The Core Prompting Framework

The Core Prompting Framework addresses the technical and structural aspects of AI communication. This pillar provides the systematic method for constructing prompts that produce consistent, professional-quality results:

- **PTCF Structure:** How to apply Persona, Task, Context, and Format components in every interaction
- **Iteration Process:** How to refine and optimize prompts based on output quality
- **Adaptation Methods:** How to modify the framework for different applications and scenarios
- **Quality Control:** How to ensure consistent results regardless of complexity

The Core Prompting Framework eliminates the guesswork and randomness that frustrates most professionals' AI attempts. It provides the technical engine that powers all advanced productivity techniques.

The Interdependence Factor

These pillars work together, not independently. The Co-Pilot Mindset without technical skills leads to strategic thinking without execution capability. The Core Prompting Framework without the right mindset leads to tactical efficiency without strategic impact.

Consider this analogy: learning to drive requires both understanding traffic principles (mindset) and mastering vehicle operation (technique). Understanding that green means go and red means stop provides strategic context, but you also need to know how to operate the steering wheel, accelerator, and brakes. Neither component alone produces driving competency.

AI productivity mastery requires the same integration. The Co-Pilot Mindset provides strategic context for how AI fits into your professional life. The Core Prompting Framework provides operational techniques for executing that strategy.

The Foundation Promise: Universal Application

Once you establish these foundations, every subsequent chapter becomes an application exercise rather than a learning challenge. Here is what this means in practical terms:

Email Automation (Chapter 2): Instead of memorizing specific email prompts, you will apply the PTCF Framework to construct prompts for any email scenario. The foundation enables adaptation rather than memorization.

Meeting Management (Chapter 3): Instead of learning separate techniques for different meeting types, you will use the Co-Pilot Mindset to identify opportunities for AI assistance and the PTCF Framework to implement those opportunities systematically.

Data Analysis (Chapter 4): Instead of struggling with technical Excel complexity, you will direct AI to perform analyses using structured prompts that translate your strategic questions into actionable insights.

Workflow Integration (Chapter 5): Instead of juggling disconnected techniques, you will orchestrate complete business processes by applying foundation principles across multiple applications simultaneously.

The Competency Acceleration Effect

Professionals who master these foundations experience accelerated skill development that compounds over time. Here is the typical progression:

Week 1-2: Foundation concepts feel abstract but begin to organize your thinking about AI productivity **Week 3-4:** First successful applications demonstrate the power of systematic approaches over random attempts **Month 2:** Complex scenarios become manageable because you understand the underlying principles **Month 3:** You begin creating original solutions by applying foundation principles to novel situations **Ongoing:** Continuous capability expansion as new AI features become additional tools in your systematic approach

The Implementation Commitment

Establishing your AI foundation requires focused attention but delivers disproportionate returns. The time investment is front-loaded, but the productivity gains compound continuously.

Foundation Building Timeline:

- **Mindset Development:** 3-4 focused sessions to internalize the Co-Pilot Mindset principles
- **Framework Mastery:** 1-2 weeks of deliberate practice with the PTCF structure
- **Integration Testing:** 1 week applying both pillars to current work scenarios

- **Optimization Period:** Ongoing refinement based on results and expanded applications

The Prerequisites Promise

This chapter contains the only prerequisites for everything that follows. You do not need technical expertise, advanced Excel skills, or extensive Microsoft 365 experience. You do not need to understand AI technology or machine learning principles.

You need exactly two things:

1. **The willingness to think differently** about your relationship with AI tools
2. **The commitment to follow a systematic process** for AI communication

These foundations will support every advanced technique, complex workflow, and strategic application covered in subsequent chapters. Invest in this foundation properly, and every other chapter becomes an implementation exercise rather than a learning struggle.

Your transformation into an AI-powered productivity professional begins with establishing the right mindset and mastering the core framework that makes consistent success possible.

1.1 The Co-Pilot Mindset

1.1.1 Moving from User to Power User

The difference between professionals who struggle with AI and those who achieve breakthrough productivity results is not technical knowledge or advanced prompting skills. The difference is mindset. Specifically, how you position yourself in relation to artificial intelligence determines whether you become more productive or simply busier.

I learned this principle while consulting for a Fortune 500 financial services firm. Two executives received identical Copilot training. Six months later, one executive had cut his report preparation time by 75% while the other had abandoned AI tools entirely, claiming they were "more trouble than they're worth." The difference was not intelligence, technical background, or available time. The difference was how each executive conceptualized their relationship with AI.

The User Versus Power User Distinction

Most professionals approach AI tools with a "user" mindset inherited from decades of traditional software interaction. This mindset creates fundamental limitations that prevent AI productivity breakthroughs.

The Traditional User Approach:

Characteristics of the Passive User:

- **Reactive Requests:** Asks AI to respond to immediate problems without strategic planning
- **Simple Commands:** Uses basic, one-sentence prompts expecting perfect results
- **Surface-Level Thinking:** Focuses on getting quick answers rather than comprehensive solutions

- **Tool Dependency:** Relies on AI to make decisions rather than providing clear direction
- **Random Experimentation:** Tries different approaches without understanding underlying principles

Typical User Interactions:

- "Summarize this email"
- "Write a report about sales"
- "Help me with this presentation"
- "Fix this document"
- "Make this better"

Predictable User Results:

- Inconsistent output quality
- Frustration with "wrong" or irrelevant responses
- Time wasted on multiple iterations
- Abandonment of AI tools due to disappointing performance
- Conclusion that AI is overhyped or not ready for professional use

The Power User Transformation

Power users approach AI with a fundamentally different mental model. They understand that artificial intelligence should augment human intelligence, not replace it. This philosophy creates a strategic relationship where the human provides direction, context, and judgment while AI handles execution, analysis, and synthesis.

Core Power User Principles:

1. Strategic Command Authority

Power users position themselves as directors who provide clear instructions rather than consumers who make vague requests.

Implementation Framework:

- **Define Objectives:** Specify exactly what you want to achieve before interacting with AI
- **Establish Parameters:** Set clear boundaries, requirements, and success criteria
- **Provide Context:** Supply relevant background information that influences the task
- **Direct Execution:** Give specific instructions about methodology and approach
- **Control Quality:** Review outputs and iterate based on strategic goals

2. Augmentation Over Automation

The critical distinction lies in understanding that AI should amplify your capabilities, not replace your thinking.

Power User Philosophy Application:

- **You Define Strategy:** AI executes tactics based on your strategic direction
- **You Provide Judgment:** AI supplies analysis for your decision-making process
- **You Set Priorities:** AI handles organization and implementation of your priorities
- **You Maintain Control:** AI operates within parameters you establish and monitor
- **You Drive Innovation:** AI supports your creative and strategic thinking processes

The Director-Assistant Dynamic

The most successful AI relationships mirror the dynamic between senior executives and their most capable assistants. The executive provides vision, priorities, and decision-making authority. The assistant handles research, analysis, drafting, and coordination.

Power User Interaction Model:

Step 1: Strategic Brief Instead of asking "Help me with this presentation," the power user provides comprehensive direction:

Power User Command Structure:

- **Role Assignment:** "Act as my executive presentation specialist"
- **Objective Definition:** "Create a quarterly review presentation for the board of directors"
- **Success Criteria:** "Focus on performance trends, strategic initiatives, and forward-looking recommendations"
- **Deliverable Specifications:** "Generate a 12-slide outline with key talking points for each section"

Step 2: Contextual Intelligence Power users supply relevant background that enables sophisticated responses:

Context Provision Framework:

- **Organizational Background:** Company priorities, strategic initiatives, recent developments
- **Audience Analysis:** Decision-makers involved, their concerns and information needs
- **Historical Context:** Previous presentations, ongoing projects, comparative timeframes
- **Performance Data:** Relevant metrics, benchmarks, and analytical requirements

Step 3: Iterative Refinement Rather than accepting first outputs, power users systematically improve results:

Refinement Process:

- **Output Evaluation:** Assess quality against defined success criteria
- **Gap Analysis:** Identify specific areas requiring improvement or modification

- **Targeted Revision:** Provide specific instructions for enhancement
- **Quality Validation:** Confirm final output meets professional standards

The Mindset Shift Implementation Plan

Transforming from user to power user requires systematic practice of new interaction patterns.

Phase 1: Relationship Redefinition (Week 1)

Daily Practice Exercises:

1. **Command Authority Training**
    - Before every AI interaction, write down your specific objective
    - Replace question-based requests with directive-based commands
    - Practice using phrases like "Create," "Analyze," "Generate," instead of "Can you help me with..."
2. **Context Awareness Development**
    - List three pieces of background information before making any request
    - Practice explaining the "why" behind each task to establish strategic context
    - Develop templates for common context categories (audience, timeframe, constraints)

Phase 2: Strategic Direction Practice (Week 2-3)

Advanced Implementation Exercises:

1. **Multi-Step Command Sequences**
    - Break complex tasks into sequential, specific instructions

- Practice chaining related requests to build comprehensive solutions
- Develop workflows that leverage AI capabilities systematically

2. Quality Control Systems

- Establish criteria for evaluating AI outputs before acceptance
- Create revision templates for common improvement areas
- Build feedback loops that improve future interactions

Phase 3: Mastery Integration (Week 4+)

Power User Capabilities Development:

1. Strategic Workflow Design

- Plan complete processes that integrate AI assistance at optimal points
- Design templates for recurring professional scenarios
- Create systems for capturing and reusing successful interaction patterns

2. Advanced Direction Techniques

- Develop persona-based commands that optimize AI performance for specific scenarios
- Master iterative refinement processes that consistently produce professional-quality results
- Build competency in adapting successful approaches to novel situations

The Augmentation Mindset in Practice

The philosophy that artificial intelligence should augment human intelligence, not replace it, translates into specific operational principles:

Human Strategic Contributions:

- **Vision Setting:** You determine what needs to be accomplished and why
- **Priority Establishment:** You decide what matters most and allocate resources accordingly
- **Judgment Application:** You evaluate options, make decisions, and provide approval
- **Relationship Management:** You handle interpersonal dynamics and stakeholder communication
- **Creative Innovation:** You generate novel approaches and strategic insights

AI Operational Contributions:

- **Information Processing:** AI handles data analysis, pattern recognition, and synthesis
- **Content Generation:** AI produces drafts, outlines, and structured materials
- **Research Execution:** AI gathers information, compares options, and organizes findings
- **Format Optimization:** AI handles formatting, organization, and presentation structure
- **Iterative Refinement:** AI modifies outputs based on your specifications and feedback

Power User Success Indicators

You have successfully adopted the power user mindset when you consistently experience these outcomes:

Productivity Measures:

- AI interactions produce usable results on first or second attempts
- Complex tasks require significantly less time while maintaining quality standards
- You can reliably delegate cognitive work to AI while retaining strategic control
- Colleagues begin asking how you achieve such efficient, high-quality outputs

Capability Measures:

- You can articulate clear instructions for sophisticated professional tasks
- You provide effective context that enables AI to deliver relevant, targeted results
- You systematically iterate and improve AI outputs to meet professional standards
- You design workflows that integrate AI assistance seamlessly into business processes

The power user mindset positions you as the strategic director of AI capabilities rather than a passive consumer of AI services. This transformation enables the augmentation philosophy that preserves human value while amplifying professional effectiveness through artificial intelligence.

1.1.2 Adopting the Augmentation Philosophy

The augmentation philosophy represents the most transformative shift you can make in your professional approach to artificial intelligence. This philosophy centers on a single, powerful principle: **artificial intelligence should amplify your uniquely human capabilities, not replace them**. When implemented correctly, this approach elevates you from task executor to strategic orchestrator, freeing your mental capacity for the work that drives real business value and career advancement.

The Executive-Chief of Staff Partnership Model

The ideal relationship between you and Microsoft 365 Copilot mirrors the partnership between a senior executive and their most capable chief of staff. I learned this principle while consulting for a Fortune 500 company whose CEO demonstrated remarkable productivity through this exact dynamic.

How the Executive-Chief of Staff Model Works:

The Executive's Role (Your Role):

- **Vision Setting:** Defines strategic objectives and long-term priorities
- **Decision Making:** Evaluates options and makes final determinations
- **Relationship Management:** Handles stakeholder interactions and negotiations
- **Creative Innovation:** Generates novel approaches and breakthrough solutions
- **Quality Control:** Reviews outputs and ensures alignment with strategic goals

The Chief of Staff's Role (Copilot's Role):

- **Information Processing:** Gathers, analyzes, and synthesizes data from multiple sources
- **Research Execution:** Investigates options, compares alternatives, and prepares recommendations
- **Draft Creation:** Produces initial versions of documents, presentations, and communications
- **Administrative Coordination:** Handles scheduling, formatting, and organizational tasks
- **Implementation Support:** Executes tactical elements of strategic decisions

Step-by-Step Implementation of the Augmentation Philosophy

Phase 1: Cognitive Load Assessment

Before delegating work to AI, you must identify which tasks consume your mental energy without contributing to your strategic value.

1. Complete a Professional Activity Audit

Document your work activities for one full week using this categorization system:

High-Value Activities (Keep These):

- Strategic planning and decision-making
- Creative problem-solving and innovation
- Stakeholder relationship building
- Team leadership and mentoring
- Client consultation and advisory work
- Complex analysis requiring judgment and experience

Low-Value Activities (Delegate These to AI):

- Email summarization and routine responses
- Document formatting and structure creation
- Data compilation and basic analysis
- Meeting agenda preparation
- Research gathering and initial synthesis
- Template-based content creation

2. Calculate Your Cognitive Opportunity Cost

For each low-value activity, estimate:

- **Time Investment:** Hours spent per week on this task
- **Mental Energy Required:** Rate from 1-10 (10 = high concentration needed)
- **Strategic Impact:** Rate from 1-10 (10 = directly drives business results)

- **Delegation Potential:** Can AI handle 80%+ of this work? (Yes/No)

Phase 2: Delegation Strategy Development

3. Apply the Executive Delegation Framework

Transform your approach to low-value tasks using these delegation principles:

Before Delegation (Traditional Approach):

- "I need to write this report myself to ensure quality"
- "I should read through this entire email thread to understand the context"
- "I have to create this presentation from scratch to get it right"

After Delegation (Augmentation Approach):

- "I will direct AI to create the first draft, then refine it with my expertise"
- "I will have AI summarize the key points, then apply my judgment to the decisions"
- "I will instruct AI to structure the presentation, then add my strategic insights"

4. Establish Your Direction-Giving Protocols

Develop systematic approaches for providing clear direction to AI:

Strategic Brief Template:

- **Objective:** What specific outcome do you want to achieve?
- **Context:** What background information affects this task?
- **Standards:** What quality criteria must the output meet?
- **Constraints:** What limitations or requirements apply?
- **Format:** How should the final deliverable be structured?

Phase 3: Human-AI Workflow Design

5. Create Hybrid Workflows for Complex Projects

Design processes that combine AI efficiency with human expertise:

Example: Strategic Report Creation Workflow

AI Handles:

1. **Research Compilation:** Gather relevant data from specified sources
2. **Initial Analysis:** Identify patterns and trends in the data
3. **Structure Creation:** Generate outline and draft sections
4. **Format Optimization:** Apply consistent formatting and visual design

You Handle:

1. **Strategic Interpretation:** Analyze what the data means for business strategy
2. **Insight Generation:** Connect findings to broader market trends and opportunities
3. **Recommendation Development:** Propose specific actions based on analysis
4. **Stakeholder Alignment:** Ensure recommendations address key decision-maker concerns

6. Implement Quality Amplification Processes

Establish systematic methods for enhancing AI outputs with your expertise:

The Enhancement Protocol:

- **AI First Draft:** Generate initial content using structured prompts
- **Strategic Review:** Evaluate alignment with business objectives and priorities
- **Expertise Integration:** Add insights, context, and judgment that only you can provide

- **Stakeholder Optimization:** Adjust content for specific audience needs and preferences
- **Final Validation:** Confirm the output meets your professional standards

Phase 4: Professional Value Elevation

7. Redirect Reclaimed Time to High-Impact Activities

Systematically invest your liberated mental capacity in work that drives measurable business value:

Strategic Thinking Allocation:

- **Monday:** 2 hours on competitive analysis and market trend evaluation
- **Wednesday:** 1.5 hours on process improvement and workflow optimization
- **Friday:** 2 hours on strategic planning and long-term project development

Relationship Building Investment:

- **Daily:** 30 minutes for meaningful stakeholder conversations
- **Weekly:** 1 hour for team mentoring and development discussions
- **Monthly:** 2 hours for cross-departmental collaboration initiatives

Innovation and Learning Focus:

- **Weekly:** 1 hour exploring new industry developments and best practices
- **Bi-weekly:** 1 hour experimenting with new approaches to existing challenges
- **Monthly:** 2 hours developing and testing innovative solutions

8. Measure Your Augmentation Impact

Track the tangible benefits of implementing the augmentation philosophy:

Productivity Metrics:

- **Time Reallocation:** Hours per week shifted from low-value to high-value work
- **Output Quality:** Improvement in deliverable sophistication and strategic depth
- **Response Speed:** Faster turnaround on routine tasks without quality reduction
- **Strategic Contribution:** Increased participation in high-level planning and decision-making

Professional Development Indicators:

- **Skill Enhancement:** New capabilities developed through increased strategic focus
- **Leadership Opportunities:** Additional responsibility and project leadership roles
- **Stakeholder Recognition:** Feedback acknowledging increased value contribution
- **Career Advancement:** Promotions, role expansions, or new opportunities

The Vision: Your Augmented Professional Future

When you fully adopt the augmentation philosophy, your professional life transforms fundamentally. You operate at a higher strategic level while maintaining operational excellence. Your days focus on innovation, relationship building, and complex problem-solving rather than administrative tasks and routine execution.

Your Augmented Workday Structure:

Morning (Strategic Focus):

- **8:00-9:30 AM:** Deep strategic work while mental energy is peak
- **9:30-10:00 AM:** AI-assisted email processing and communication management
- **10:00-11:00 AM:** Stakeholder meetings and relationship development

Midday (Creative and Collaborative Work):

- **11:00-12:00 PM:** Problem-solving sessions and innovative thinking
- **1:00-2:30 PM:** Team leadership and collaborative project work
- **2:30-3:00 PM:** AI-assisted document review and content refinement

Afternoon (Implementation and Planning):

- **3:00-4:00 PM:** Strategic planning and future-focused analysis
- **4:00-5:00 PM:** AI-supported research and competitive intelligence gathering
- **5:00-5:30 PM:** Priority setting and next-day strategic planning

This augmented approach positions you as a strategic professional who leverages artificial intelligence to amplify your human capabilities while preserving and enhancing your unique value contribution to the organization.

1.2 The Core Prompting Framework

1.2.1 Constructing Prompts with Persona, Task, Context, and Format (PTCF)

The PTCF Framework transforms chaotic AI interactions into systematic, professional-quality results. This four-component structure provides the technical foundation for every successful prompt you will create throughout your Microsoft 365 Copilot journey. Master these components, and you will never struggle with inconsistent AI outputs again.

The PTCF Framework Components Overview

Each letter in PTCF represents a critical element that must be present in every professional prompt:

- **P - Persona:** Defines the AI's professional role and expertise level
- **T - Task:** Specifies the exact action you want the AI to perform
- **C - Context:** Provides essential background information for informed responses
- **F - Format:** Dictates how you want the output structured and presented

Component 1: Persona (P) - Establishing AI Professional Identity

The Persona component assigns a specific professional role to the AI, fundamentally changing how it processes information and structures responses.

Why Persona Matters:

- **Response Quality:** Different professional roles organize information differently

- **Language Style:** A CFO communicates differently than a project coordinator
- **Priority Focus:** Each role emphasizes different aspects of the same information
- **Decision Framework:** Professional roles apply different evaluation criteria

Persona Construction Elements:

1. **Professional Title**

    - Be specific: "Act as a project manager" not "Act as a manager"
    - Include seniority when relevant: "Act as a senior financial analyst"
    - Add specialization: "Act as a marketing manager specializing in B2B software"

2. **Industry Context**

    - Include when it affects approach: "Act as a project manager in healthcare"
    - Specify regulatory environment: "Act as a compliance officer in financial services"
    - Reference company size: "Act as an operations director at a Fortune 500 company"

Persona Examples:

- **Basic:** "Act as a project manager"
- **Enhanced:** "Act as a senior project manager in the technology sector"
- **Advanced:** "Act as an experienced project manager specializing in software implementation for enterprise clients"

Component 2: Task (T) - Defining Precise Objectives

The Task component eliminates ambiguity by specifying exactly what you want the AI to accomplish.

Task Specification Requirements:

1. **Action Verb Selection**

    - **Analysis Tasks:** Analyze, evaluate, assess, compare, identify
    - **Creation Tasks:** Create, generate, draft, develop, design
    - **Processing Tasks:** Summarize, organize, categorize, prioritize, consolidate

2. **Scope Definition**

    - **What to include:** "Analyze the Q3 sales data focusing on regional performance"
    - **What to exclude:** "Summarize this report excluding the technical appendices"
    - **Depth level:** "Provide a high-level overview" vs "Conduct detailed analysis"

3. **Success Criteria**

    - **Quality standards:** "Create a professional presentation suitable for board review"
    - **Completeness requirements:** "Include all major risk factors and mitigation strategies"
    - **Accuracy specifications:** "Ensure all financial calculations are precise"

Task Examples:

- **Vague:** "Help with this email"
- **Improved:** "Draft a professional email response"
- **Optimal:** "Draft a professional follow-up email requesting the overdue quarterly budget report, maintaining a firm but respectful tone"

Component 3: Context (C) - Supplying Essential Background

Context provides the AI with relevant information needed to produce informed, appropriate responses.

Context Categories and Applications:

1. **Situational Background**

    - **Current circumstances:** "This is for an emergency board meeting called due to budget overruns"
    - **Timeline pressure:** "We need this completed before the client presentation tomorrow"
    - **Stakeholder dynamics:** "The client has been frustrated with previous delays"

2. **Organizational Information**

    - **Company details:** "We are a mid-sized manufacturing company"
    - **Department context:** "This is for the marketing department's quarterly review"
    - **Cultural considerations:** "Our company culture emphasizes data-driven decisions"

3. **Historical Context**

    - **Previous interactions:** "This follows up on last month's strategic planning session"
    - **Past performance:** "Our Q2 results exceeded expectations by 15%"
    - **Ongoing initiatives:** "This relates to our digital transformation project"

4. **Audience Information**

    - **Recipients:** "This will be presented to the executive leadership team"
    - **Knowledge level:** "The audience has limited technical background"

- **Decision authority:** "These stakeholders will approve the budget allocation"

Context Implementation Strategy:

- **Lead with most important information:** Priority context first
- **Include decision-relevant details:** Information that affects approach or conclusions
- **Exclude irrelevant background:** Focus on details that impact the task

Component 4: Format (F) - Specifying Output Structure

Format ensures your results are immediately usable without additional processing.

Format Specification Options:

1. **Document Structure**
   - **Email format:** "Structure as a professional business email with clear subject line"
   - **Report layout:** "Organize as an executive summary with key findings and recommendations"
   - **List format:** "Present as a numbered priority list with brief explanations"
2. **Length Requirements**
   - **Word limits:** "Keep the summary under 200 words"
   - **Section counts:** "Provide exactly 5 key recommendations"
   - **Time specifications:** "Create talking points for a 10-minute presentation"
3. **Visual Organization**
   - **Heading structure:** "Use clear headings and subheadings for easy scanning"

- **Table format:** "Present findings in a three-column comparison table"
- **Bullet organization:** "Structure as bulleted action items with deadlines"

4. **Audience Adaptation**

    - **Formality level:** "Use formal business language appropriate for board communication"
    - **Technical depth:** "Write for a non-technical executive audience"
    - **Cultural tone:** "Maintain a collaborative, solution-focused tone"

Complete PTCF Template

Here is your master template for constructing professional prompts:

```
None
**Persona:** Act as a [specific professional role + seniority + specialization/industry]


**Task:** [Action verb] + [specific objective] + [scope/constraints] + [success criteria]


**Context:** [Most important background information] + [stakeholder details] + [situational factors] + [organizational context]


**Format:** [Structure type] + [length requirements] + [visual organization] + [audience considerations]
```

PTCF Framework in Action: Complete Example

Scenario: You need to create a project status update for your manager.

Step 1: Apply the PTCF Template

```
None
Persona: Act as an experienced project manager in
the technology sector


Task: Create a comprehensive project status update
that summarizes current progress, identifies key
risks, and provides clear next steps for the
customer onboarding system implementation


Context: This is for my manager who needs to update
the executive team tomorrow. The project is
currently 2 weeks behind schedule due to
integration challenges with the legacy system. The
client is concerned about the delay but remains
committed. We have identified solutions but need
additional resources.


Format: Structure as a professional email with
clear sections: Executive Summary (2-3 sentences),
Current Status (bulleted progress points), Key
Risks & Issues (numbered list with mitigation
plans), Next Steps (prioritized action items with
owners and dates). Keep the total length under 300
words for quick executive review.
```

Step 2: Implement the Complete Prompt

Copy and paste this complete prompt into Microsoft 365 Copilot:

```
Act as an experienced project manager in the
technology sector. Create a comprehensive project
status update that summarizes current progress,
identifies key risks, and provides clear next steps
for the customer onboarding system implementation.
This is for my manager who needs to update the
executive team tomorrow. The project is currently 2
weeks behind schedule due to integration challenges
with the legacy system. The client is concerned
about the delay but remains committed. We have
identified solutions but need additional resources.
Structure as a professional email with clear
sections: Executive Summary (2-3 sentences),
Current Status (bulleted progress points), Key
Risks & Issues (numbered list with mitigation
plans), Next Steps (prioritized action items with
owners and dates). Keep the total length under 300
words for quick executive review.
```

PTCF Implementation Checklist

Before sending any prompt to Copilot, verify each component:

✓ Persona Check:

- Have I specified a clear professional role?
- Is the expertise level appropriate for the task?
- Does the role match the type of work requested?

✓ Task Check:

- Did I use a specific action verb?
- Are the objectives clearly defined?
- Have I included success criteria?

✓ **Context Check:**

- Does the AI have sufficient background information?
- Have I included relevant stakeholder details?
- Is the situational context clear?

✓ **Format Check:**

- Have I specified the desired structure?
- Are length requirements included?
- Is the audience's consideration addressed?

The PTCF Framework eliminates guesswork from AI interactions and ensures consistent, professional results across all Microsoft 365 Copilot applications. This systematic approach becomes the foundation for every advanced technique you will learn in subsequent chapters.

1.2.2 THE ART OF ITERATION: REFINING PROMPTS FOR PRECISION

Perfect prompts do not emerge fully formed on the first attempt. The most successful AI productivity professionals understand that prompt refinement follows a systematic process of evaluation, diagnosis, and strategic adjustment. This iterative approach transforms mediocre AI outputs into professional-quality results that meet your exact specifications.

The Iteration Principle: First Draft to Final Excellence

Most professionals abandon AI tools after receiving disappointing results from their initial prompts. They conclude that AI cannot meet professional standards rather than recognizing that their prompting technique requires refinement. This represents a fundamental misunderstanding of how AI productivity mastery develops.

Professional prompt iteration follows a predictable pattern:

- **Initial Attempt:** First prompt generates directionally correct but incomplete results
- **Gap Analysis:** Systematic evaluation identifies specific improvement opportunities
- **Strategic Refinement:** Targeted adjustments to PTCF components address identified gaps
- **Quality Validation:** Revised prompt produces professional-standard output
- **Pattern Recognition:** Successful refinements become templates for future scenarios

The Five-Step Iteration Process

Step 1: Execute Your Initial Prompt

Begin with your best application of the PTCF Framework based on current information. Accept that this represents a starting point, not a final solution.

Step 2: Conduct Output Gap Analysis

Systematically evaluate the AI response against professional requirements:

Content Quality Assessment:

- **Completeness:** Does the output address all required elements?
- **Accuracy:** Are facts, data, and logic correct and verifiable?
- **Relevance:** Does the content directly serve the stated objective?
- **Professional Standards:** Does the quality meet workplace expectations?

Format and Structure Evaluation:

- **Organization:** Is information logically sequenced and clearly structured?
- **Scannability:** Can busy professionals quickly find key information?
- **Consistency:** Does formatting match professional document standards?
- **Audience Appropriateness:** Is language and detail level suitable for intended recipients?

Step 3: Diagnose PTCF Component Weaknesses

Map identified gaps to specific PTCF framework elements:

Persona Issues:

- Generic or inappropriate professional voice
- Wrong expertise level for the task complexity
- Mismatch between role and expected output style

Task Problems:

- Vague or ambiguous action requests
- Missing success criteria or quality specifications
- Unclear scope boundaries or deliverable expectations

Context Gaps:

- Insufficient background information for informed responses
- Missing stakeholder or situational details
- Inadequate organizational or industry context

Format Deficiencies:

- Unspecified structure requirements
- Missing length or organization parameters
- Unclear audience adaptation needs

Step 4: Apply Strategic PTCF Refinements

Enhance each problematic component with specific, targeted improvements:

Persona Enhancement Techniques:

- Add seniority level: "senior project manager" instead of "project manager"
- Include specialization: "marketing manager specializing in B2B software"
- Specify industry context: "financial services compliance officer"

Task Precision Methods:

- Use specific action verbs: "analyze and recommend" instead of "help with"
- Define success criteria: "suitable for board presentation"
- Set clear boundaries: "focusing on Q3 results excluding technical details"

Context Expansion Strategies:

- Add stakeholder information: "for executive team review"
- Include situational factors: "due to budget constraints"
- Provide decision context: "to support vendor selection process"

Format Specification Improvements:

- Define structure: "organized as executive summary with bulleted recommendations"
- Set length parameters: "maximum 300 words for quick review"
- Specify audience adaptation: "technical complexity appropriate for non-engineering managers"

Step 5: Validate and Document Successful Patterns

Test refined prompts and capture successful refinement patterns for future application.

Complete Iteration Example: Project Status Update

Initial Prompt (Inadequate):

```
None
Help me write a project update.
```

Initial Output (Mediocre Result): *Generic, unhelpful response about project updates in general rather than creating specific content*

Gap Analysis Results:

- **Persona:** No professional role specified
- **Task:** Vague request with no clear deliverable
- **Context:** Zero background information provided
- **Format:** No structure or audience requirements

Refined Prompt (PTCF Applied):

```
None
Act as an experienced project manager in the
technology sector. Create a comprehensive project
status update for the customer onboarding system
implementation project. This update is for my
manager who needs to brief the executive team
tomorrow morning. The project is currently 2 weeks
behind the original timeline due to unexpected
integration challenges with our legacy billing
system. The development team has identified a
solution that requires 3 additional weeks and one
extra senior developer. The client is aware of the
```

```
delay and remains committed to the project.
Structure this as a professional email with clear
sections: Executive Summary (2-3 sentences),
Current Status (bulleted progress points), Key
Issues & Resolutions (numbered list), Next Steps
(prioritized action items with owners and
timeline). Keep the total length under 350 words
for executive consumption.
```

Refined Output (Professional Quality):

Subject: Customer Onboarding System - Status Update & Resource Request

Executive Summary: The customer onboarding system implementation is currently 2 weeks behind schedule due to legacy system integration complexity. We have identified a technical solution requiring 3 additional weeks and one senior developer to maintain project quality and client satisfaction.

Current Status:

- User interface development: 85% complete (on track)
- Database design and setup: 90% complete (ahead of schedule)
- Legacy billing system integration: 40% complete (behind schedule due to undocumented API limitations)
- User acceptance testing framework: 70% complete (on track)

Key Issues & Resolutions:

1. **Legacy Integration Challenge:** Billing system API documentation incomplete, requiring reverse engineering

Resolution: Senior developer with legacy system expertise to join team for 3-week sprint

2. **Timeline Impact:** Original delivery date no longer achievable with quality standards **Resolution:** Revised timeline adds 3 weeks while maintaining all functionality requirements

Next Steps:

1. **Immediate (This Week):** Secure senior developer resource approval - *Owner: Project Manager*
2. **Week 2:** Complete legacy system analysis and integration planning - *Owner: Tech Lead*
3. **Weeks 3-5:** Execute integration development with expanded team - *Owner: Development Team*
4. **Week 6:** Conduct comprehensive testing and client review - *Owner: QA Team*

The client relationship remains strong, and this approach ensures we deliver a robust solution that meets their long-term needs.

Analysis of Improvement Achieved

The refined prompt using complete PTCF framework produced:

Professional Completeness:

- All essential project status elements included
- Clear executive summary for quick decision-making
- Specific progress metrics and timeline projections

Strategic Communication:

- Positions challenges within solution context
- Demonstrates proactive problem management
- Maintains confidence while requesting resources

Actionable Organization:

- Scannable structure for busy executives
- Clear ownership and timeline assignments
- Professional email format ready for immediate use

Common Iteration Patterns

Pattern 1: Persona Upgrading

- **Initial:** "Act as a manager"
- **Refined:** "Act as a senior operations manager in manufacturing with 10+ years of supply chain experience"

Pattern 2: Task Precision Enhancement

- **Initial:** "Write a report"
- **Refined:** "Create a comprehensive quarterly performance analysis with specific recommendations for process improvement"

Pattern 3: Context Expansion

- **Initial:** "This is for my boss"
- **Refined:** "This is for the VP of Operations who needs to present findings to the board next week, focusing on cost reduction opportunities"

Pattern 4: Format Specification

- **Initial:** "Make it professional"
- **Refined:** "Structure as a formal business memo with executive summary, three main findings, and specific recommendations, maximum 500 words"

Building Iteration Confidence

Prompt refinement becomes intuitive through systematic practice. Each iteration cycle teaches you to:

1. **Recognize Quality Gaps Quickly:** Develop ability to immediately identify missing elements in AI outputs

2. **Diagnose PTCF Weaknesses:** Map output problems to specific framework components requiring adjustment
3. **Apply Targeted Refinements:** Make surgical improvements rather than completely rewriting prompts
4. **Validate Professional Standards:** Ensure final outputs meet workplace quality expectations

The iteration process transforms from debugging exercise into strategic AI direction technique. You develop confidence in your ability to guide AI toward precise, professional results that serve your specific business objectives.

Your mastery of prompt iteration establishes the technical foundation for all advanced Microsoft 365 Copilot applications covered in subsequent chapters.

2. Automate Your Communications

You now possess the Co-Pilot Mindset and understand the PTCF Framework. These foundations represent the essential prerequisites for AI productivity mastery. The mindset positions you as a strategic director of artificial intelligence, while the framework provides the systematic structure for communicating your intentions clearly and consistently.

This chapter marks the transition from understanding the system to implementing it in your daily professional life. You will apply the PTCF Framework to the two most time-consuming communication activities in modern work: email management and document creation.

The Communication Time Trap

Email and document creation consume approximately 40% of the average professional's workday. I have observed this pattern consistently across every organization I have advised, from Fortune 500 corporations to mid-sized consulting firms. The time allocation breaks down as follows:

- **Email Processing:** 2.5 hours per day managing inbox, reading threads, and composing responses
- **Document Creation:** 1.5 hours per day drafting reports, memos, proposals, and presentations
- **Communication Overhead:** 30 minutes per day formatting, editing, and coordinating communication workflows

This represents 4 hours of your 8-hour workday dedicated to communication tasks rather than strategic, value-creating work. The productivity cost extends beyond time investment. Communication tasks fragment your attention, interrupt deep work sessions, and create cognitive switching costs that reduce your effectiveness throughout the entire day.

The Amplification Opportunity

Most professionals approach email and document creation as necessary administrative burdens. This perspective fundamentally misunderstands the strategic opportunity these activities represent when augmented with AI capabilities.

Communication tasks follow predictable patterns that make them ideal candidates for AI augmentation:

Pattern Recognition Advantages:

- **Structured Formats:** Emails and documents follow established business communication conventions
- **Repetitive Elements:** Many communications contain similar information organized in familiar ways
- **Clear Objectives:** Each communication serves a specific purpose that can be systematically defined
- **Measurable Outcomes:** Communication effectiveness can be evaluated based on recipient response and task completion

AI Augmentation Benefits:

- **Speed Acceleration:** AI generates initial drafts 10-15 times faster than manual writing
- **Consistency Improvement:** Systematic prompting ensures professional quality across all communications
- **Cognitive Load Reduction:** AI handles structure and formatting while you focus on strategic content

- **Quality Enhancement:** AI can adapt tone, style, and complexity for different audiences instantly

When you master AI-augmented communication, you transform these time-consuming activities into strategic advantages. Your email responses become more thoughtful and comprehensive. Your documents achieve higher professional standards. Most importantly, you reclaim 3-4 hours per day for high-value work that advances your career and creates business impact.

Chapter Implementation Strategy

This chapter introduces two interconnected systems that leverage the PTCF Framework for communication mastery:

System 1: The Zero-Inbox System

The Zero-Inbox System applies the PTCF Framework to email management using Microsoft Outlook Copilot. This system addresses the two most challenging aspects of professional email:

Email Thread Summarization: You will learn to construct prompts that instantly digest long, complex email conversations into clear, actionable summaries. Instead of spending 15-20 minutes reading through a 30-message thread to understand current status, you will generate comprehensive summaries in under 2 minutes.

Strategic Email Composition: You will master prompt structures that generate professional, contextually appropriate email responses for any business scenario. Whether you need to decline a request diplomatically, follow up on overdue deliverables, or respond to complex client inquiries, you will have systematic prompt templates that produce high-quality results consistently.

System 2: The Instant Document Drafter

The Instant Document Drafter applies the PTCF Framework to document creation using Microsoft Word Copilot. This system transforms the document creation process from time-intensive writing to strategic editing and refinement:

First Draft Generation: You will learn to construct prompts that generate complete first drafts of business documents including reports, memos, proposals, and policy announcements. These prompts eliminate the "blank page" challenge and provide structured, professional foundations for any document type.

Tone and Audience Adaptation: You will master prompt techniques that modify existing content for different audiences and communication objectives. A single document can be adapted for executive review, team implementation, client presentation, or regulatory compliance using specific prompt sequences.

The Integration Advantage

These systems work synergistically to create compound productivity benefits. Email communications often generate document requirements. Document creation frequently requires email coordination and distribution. When you master both systems using the same PTCF Framework, you develop workflow efficiency that extends far beyond individual task optimization.

Workflow Integration Examples:

- **Project Updates:** Summarize email project discussions, then generate status report documents, then draft distribution emails
- **Client Communications:** Process client inquiry emails, create detailed response documents, then compose professional cover emails
- **Meeting Coordination:** Generate meeting agendas from email threads, create pre-meeting briefing documents, then distribute preparation emails

The Transformation Promise

By the end of this chapter, you will handle your professional communications in a fraction of the current time while achieving superior quality and consistency. Specifically, you will:

Time Reduction Achievements:

- **Email Processing:** Reduce daily email time from 2.5 hours to 45 minutes through systematic summarization and response generation
- **Document Creation:** Reduce document drafting time from 1.5 hours to 30 minutes through structured first-draft generation and targeted refinement
- **Communication Coordination:** Eliminate 30 minutes of daily formatting and editing through consistent prompt-based workflows

Quality Enhancement Outcomes:

- **Professional Consistency:** All communications maintain professional standards regardless of time pressure or workload
- **Strategic Focus:** Communication content addresses core business objectives rather than administrative details
- **Audience Optimization:** Messages are automatically adapted for recipient context and communication purpose

Cognitive Liberation Results:

- **Reduced Decision Fatigue:** Systematic prompts eliminate micro-decisions about phrasing, structure, and formatting
- **Increased Mental Availability:** Reclaimed cognitive capacity available for strategic thinking and creative problem-solving
- **Enhanced Professional Confidence:** Consistent, high-quality communication output builds reputation and career advancement opportunities

Implementation Prerequisites

You have already established the essential foundations for communication automation success. The Co-Pilot Mindset positions you as the strategic director who provides clear instructions and maintains quality control. The PTCF Framework gives you the technical structure for constructing effective prompts consistently.

The communication applications in this chapter represent direct implementations of these foundations rather than entirely new concepts. Each prompt you will learn follows the Persona, Task, Context, Format structure you have already mastered. Each interaction applies the augmentation philosophy of delegating structured work to AI while maintaining human strategic oversight.

Your role evolves from communication composer to communication director. You define objectives, provide context, and ensure quality while Microsoft 365 Copilot handles drafting, formatting, and structural organization. This transformation enables the strategic, high-impact professional work that drives career advancement and business results.

The systems you will master in this chapter provide the practical foundation for every advanced AI productivity technique covered in subsequent chapters.

2.1 THE ZERO-INBOX SYSTEM

2.1.1 SUMMARIZING LONG EMAIL THREADS INSTANTLY

Email threads represent one of the most significant productivity drains in professional communication. A single thread can span dozens of messages, multiple participants, and several weeks of discussion. Reading through these conversations to extract key information wastes valuable time and creates cognitive overload that reduces your strategic effectiveness.

I have observed professionals spend 15-20 minutes reading through complex email threads, often missing critical decisions or action items buried within the conversation. This inefficiency compounds throughout the day, consuming hours that could be dedicated to high-impact work.

The PTCF Framework transforms email thread processing from time-intensive reading to strategic information extraction. You will master specific prompt structures that enable Microsoft Outlook Copilot to digest complex conversations and deliver precisely the information you need in the format that serves your immediate objectives.

Core Principles of Thread Summarization

Effective email thread summarization requires systematic prompt construction that addresses four critical elements:

- **Information Extraction:** Identifying key decisions, action items, and unresolved issues
- **Participant Tracking:** Understanding who contributed what information and commitments
- **Timeline Clarity:** Establishing chronological progression of decisions and developments
- **Actionable Output:** Producing results that enable immediate next steps

The Thread Analysis Categories

Email thread summarization serves different business purposes requiring distinct prompt approaches. You will master five essential categories:

1. **Executive Overview Summaries**
2. **Decision Tracking Summaries**
3. **Action Item Extraction**
4. **Project Status Summaries**
5. **Issue Resolution Tracking**

Category 1: Executive Overview Summaries

Executive overview summaries provide high-level thread comprehension for busy stakeholders who need strategic context without operational details.

Core Prompt Structure:

```
None
Persona: Act as an executive assistant to a senior manager

Task: Create a comprehensive but concise summary of this email thread

Context: This summary will be used to brief executives who need to understand the current situation quickly

Format: Structure as a 3-paragraph summary: Situation Overview, Key Developments, Current Status
```

Ready-to-Use Executive Summary Prompt:

```
None
Act as an executive assistant to a senior manager.
Create a comprehensive but concise summary of this
email thread that will be used to brief executives
who need to understand the current situation
quickly. Structure as a 3-paragraph summary:
Situation Overview (what the thread is about and
why it matters), Key Developments (major points of
discussion and any decisions made), and Current
Status (where things stand now and what happens
next). Keep the total length under 200 words and
focus on information that would matter to someone
making strategic decisions.
```

Category 2: Decision Tracking Summaries

Decision tracking summaries identify all choices made during the conversation, who made them, and their implications for ongoing work.

Core Prompt Structure:

```
None
Persona: Act as a project coordinator focused on
decision documentation

Task: Extract and organize all decisions made in
this email thread

Context: This will be used to maintain accurate
project records and ensure accountability

Format: Present as a numbered list with decision,
decision maker, and date for each item
```

Ready-to-Use Decision Tracking Prompt:

> None
>
> Act as a project coordinator focused on decision documentation. Extract and organize all decisions made in this email thread for use in maintaining accurate project records and ensuring accountability. Present as a numbered list with the following format for each decision: 1) Decision Made: [clear statement of what was decided], 2) Decision Maker: [person who made or approved the decision], 3) Date/Timestamp: [when the decision was communicated], 4) Impact: [brief note on what this decision affects]. If no formal decisions were made, state "No formal decisions identified in this thread."

Category 3: Action Item Extraction

Action item extraction identifies all tasks, assignments, and commitments generated during the email conversation.

Core Prompt Structure:

> None
>
> Persona: Act as a task management specialist
>
> Task: Create a complete list of all action items from this email thread
>
> Context: This will be used to update project tracking systems and follow up on commitments

Format: Present as a table with columns for Task, Owner, Deadline, and Status

Ready-to-Use Action Item Extraction Prompt:

None

Act as a task management specialist. Create a complete list of all action items from this email thread for use in updating project tracking systems and following up on commitments. Present as a table with these columns: Task Description (specific action to be taken), Assigned Owner (person responsible), Deadline (if mentioned, otherwise note "No deadline specified"), Dependencies (what needs to happen first), and Current Status (based on latest emails). Include both explicit assignments ("John will handle the budget analysis") and implied commitments ("I'll look into the vendor options"). If no action items are identified, state "No action items found in this thread."

Category 4: Project Status Summaries

Project status summaries synthesize progress updates, challenges, and next steps from ongoing project discussions.

Core Prompt Structure:

None

Persona: Act as a project manager preparing status reports

Task: Synthesize project status information from this email thread

Context: This will be used to update stakeholders on current project progress

Format: Organize as Progress Made, Current Challenges, Next Steps, and Timeline Updates

Ready-to-Use Project Status Summary Prompt:

None

Act as a project manager preparing status reports. Synthesize project status information from this email thread for use in updating stakeholders on current project progress. Organize as four sections: 1) Progress Made (what has been accomplished since the last update), 2) Current Challenges (obstacles, delays, or issues being discussed), 3) Next Steps (immediate actions planned), and 4) Timeline Updates (any changes to deadlines or milestones). For each section, include specific details mentioned in the emails and identify who provided the information. If the thread doesn't contain project status information, state which type of information is missing.

Category 5: Issue Resolution Tracking

Issue resolution tracking follows problems from identification through resolution, documenting all proposed solutions and their outcomes.

Core Prompt Structure:

```
None
Persona: Act as a problem-solving coordinator

Task: Track issue resolution progress throughout
this email thread

Context: This will be used to document
problem-solving approaches and outcomes

Format: Structure as Issue Description, Proposed
Solutions, Decision Made, and Resolution Status
```

Ready-to-Use Issue Resolution Tracking Prompt:

```
None
Act as a problem-solving coordinator. Track issue
resolution progress throughout this email thread
for use in documenting problem-solving approaches
and outcomes. Structure as four sections: 1) Issue
Description (what problem is being addressed and
why it matters), 2) Proposed Solutions (all options
discussed with who suggested each), 3) Decision
Made (which solution was chosen and who made the
decision), and 4) Resolution Status (current
implementation progress or outcome). Include
timeline information where available and note any
outstanding concerns or unresolved aspects. If
multiple issues are discussed, address each
separately.
```

Implementation Instructions

Step 1: Access Outlook Copilot

1. Open Microsoft Outlook in your desktop application or web browser
2. Navigate to the email thread you want to summarize
3. Look for the Copilot icon in the Outlook interface (typically in the toolbar area)
4. Click on the Copilot icon to open the AI assistant panel

Step 2: Select Appropriate Prompt

1. Determine your summarization objective from the five categories above
2. Copy the corresponding ready-to-use prompt from this section
3. Paste the prompt into the Copilot chat interface
4. Ensure the email thread is selected or referenced

Step 3: Execute and Refine

1. Send the prompt to Copilot
2. Review the generated summary
3. If the output needs adjustment, use iteration techniques:
   - Add specific requirements: "Also include budget discussions"
   - Modify format: "Present as bullet points instead of paragraphs"
   - Adjust scope: "Focus only on decisions made in the last week"

Step 4: Apply Output Immediately

1. Copy the generated summary to your preferred location
2. Use the information for immediate next steps:
   - Forward executive summaries to stakeholders

- Add action items to task management systems
- Update project documentation with status information
- Schedule follow-ups for unresolved issues

Quick Win Testing Protocol

Start with this immediate implementation sequence to experience the productivity benefits:

Test 1: Executive Summary (5 minutes)

1. Select a recent email thread with 8+ messages
2. Use the Executive Summary prompt exactly as written
3. Compare the AI summary time (under 2 minutes) vs. manual reading time (10+ minutes)
4. Verify the summary captures all key points you remember

Test 2: Action Item Extraction (5 minutes)

1. Choose an email thread containing task assignments or commitments
2. Apply the Action Item Extraction prompt
3. Cross-reference the AI output with your manual identification of tasks
4. Use the generated list to update your task management system

Test 3: Decision Tracking (5 minutes)

1. Find an email thread where decisions were made
2. Execute the Decision Tracking prompt
3. Confirm all decisions are captured accurately
4. Share the formatted decision log with relevant stakeholders

These test scenarios provide immediate validation of the system's effectiveness while building your confidence in prompt-based email management. Each successful test demonstrates measurable time savings and improved information accuracy compared to manual email processing.

You now possess systematic prompts that transform overwhelming email threads into organized, actionable information, reclaiming hours of productive time for strategic work priorities.

2.1.2 Drafting High-Impact Replies in Seconds

Professional email composition represents one of the most time-consuming and mentally draining aspects of modern work communication. The average professional spends 45 minutes daily composing email responses, often struggling with tone, structure, and completeness. Each response requires strategic thinking about audience, context, and desired outcomes, creating decision fatigue that accumulates throughout the day.

The PTCF Framework transforms email composition from lengthy, stressful writing sessions into systematic, 30-second prompt executions. You will master structured approaches that generate contextually appropriate, professionally polished responses for any business scenario while maintaining your authentic voice and strategic objectives.

The Strategic Email Response Categories

Professional email responses serve five primary business functions, each requiring distinct prompt approaches:

- **Polite Declinations:** Professional refusals that maintain relationships
- **Follow-Up Communications:** Progress requests and deadline reminders
- **Client Inquiry Responses:** Comprehensive answers to customer questions

- **Internal Coordination:** Team updates and project communications
- **Stakeholder Updates:** Status reports and strategic briefings

Category 1: Polite Declinations

Polite declinations require delicate balance between firm boundaries and relationship preservation. The PTCF Framework ensures consistent professionalism while avoiding common pitfalls like over-explanation or unclear messaging.

Core Prompt Structure Analysis:

```
None
Persona: Act as a diplomatic professional
maintaining positive relationships

Task: Decline the request while offering
alternative value when possible

Context: Preserve long-term relationship and leave
door open for future collaboration

Format: Brief, respectful, and definitive response
with clear next steps
```

Ready-to-Use Polite Declination Prompt:

```
None
Act as a diplomatic business professional who
values relationships and clear communication.
Decline the request mentioned in this email thread
while maintaining a positive, respectful tone.
Provide a brief explanation for the decision
```

```
without over-justifying, and offer an alternative
suggestion or future possibility where appropriate.
Structure the response as: 1) Acknowledgment of the
request, 2) Clear but polite declination, 3) Brief
reason (optional), 4) Alternative suggestion or
future consideration, 5) Positive closing that
maintains the relationship. Keep the tone
professional, direct, and gracious. Length should
be 3-4 sentences maximum.
```

Why This Prompt Works:

- **Persona Selection:** "Diplomatic business professional" establishes the appropriate balance between firmness and relationship maintenance
- **Task Specification:** Clear directive to decline while providing alternatives prevents ambiguous responses
- **Context Integration:** Relationship preservation focus ensures long-term strategic thinking
- **Format Definition:** Structured approach prevents rambling or unclear messaging

Category 2: Follow-Up Communications

Follow-up emails require persistent professionalism without appearing pushy or demanding. These prompts generate responses that maintain momentum while respecting recipient workload and constraints.

Core Prompt Structure Analysis:

None

Persona: Act as an organized project coordinator focused on results

Task: Request status update or action while maintaining collaborative tone

Context: Balance urgency with respect for recipient's time and priorities

Format: Concise request with clear expectations and timeline

Ready-to-Use Follow-Up Communication Prompt:

None

Act as an organized and collaborative project coordinator. Create a professional follow-up email regarding the outstanding item mentioned in this thread. Reference the specific request or deadline from previous communications and inquire about current status or any obstacles. Maintain a helpful, solution-focused tone that shows understanding of competing priorities. Structure as: 1) Brief reference to original request and timeline, 2) Polite status inquiry, 3) Offer of assistance or resources if needed, 4) Clear next steps or revised timeline request. Keep the tone cooperative and professional, avoiding any language that could seem demanding or impatient.

Why This Prompt Works:

- **Persona Choice:** "Organized project coordinator" conveys competence without authority overreach
- **Task Balance:** Combines persistence with collaboration to maintain working relationships
- **Context Awareness:** Acknowledges recipient priorities while advancing project needs
- **Format Clarity:** Structured approach ensures all necessary elements without redundancy

Category 3: Client Inquiry Responses

Client inquiry responses require comprehensive information delivery while maintaining professional expertise and helpfulness. These prompts ensure completeness while avoiding overwhelming technical detail.

Core Prompt Structure Analysis:

```
None
Persona: Act as a knowledgeable customer service
professional and subject matter expert

Task: Provide comprehensive answer while addressing
underlying concerns

Context: Build client confidence and demonstrate
organizational competence

Format: Well-organized response with clear action
items and next steps
```

Ready-to-Use Client Inquiry Response Prompt:

```
None
Act as a knowledgeable customer service
professional and subject matter expert in this
field. Create a comprehensive response to the
client inquiry in this email thread, addressing
both the explicit question and any underlying
concerns that may be implied. Use information from
the previous email exchanges to provide
context-aware answers. Structure the response as:
1) Acknowledgment of their specific question or
concern, 2) Clear, detailed answer using
non-technical language appropriate for the client,
3) Additional relevant information they should
know, 4) Specific next steps with timelines, 5)
Invitation for follow-up questions. Maintain a
helpful, professional tone that demonstrates
expertise while being accessible. Include
references to previous discussions when relevant to
show attentiveness.
```

Why This Prompt Works:

- **Persona Combination:** Dual expertise ensures both service quality and technical accuracy
- **Task Comprehensiveness:** Addresses explicit and implicit needs for thorough customer satisfaction
- **Context Integration:** References previous exchanges to demonstrate attention and continuity
- **Format Organization:** Structured approach ensures no critical information is omitted

Category 4: Internal Coordination

Internal coordination emails require clear, actionable communication that facilitates team productivity and project advancement. These prompts generate responses that eliminate ambiguity and streamline collaboration.

Core Prompt Structure Analysis:

```
None
Persona: Act as an efficient team member focused on
project success

Task: Coordinate activities and ensure clear
communication of responsibilities

Context: Support team productivity and eliminate
potential confusion

Format: Clear, scannable response with specific
details and timelines
```

Ready-to-Use Internal Coordination Prompt:

```
None
Act as an efficient team member focused on project
success and clear communication. Create a
coordinating response that addresses the team
communication in this email thread. Provide
specific information, clarify any ambiguities, and
ensure all team members have the details needed to
move forward effectively. Structure as: 1) Summary
of current situation or decision, 2) Specific
information or updates relevant to the discussion,
3) Clear action items with assigned
responsibilities and deadlines, 4) Any dependencies
or coordination requirements, 5) Next meeting or
```

```
check-in timing if applicable. Use a collaborative,
professional tone that facilitates team
productivity. Make all details specific and
actionable to prevent follow-up confusion.
```

Why This Prompt Works:

- **Persona Focus:** Team-oriented approach ensures collaborative rather than directive tone
- **Task Clarity:** Emphasizes elimination of ambiguity for improved team efficiency
- **Context Priority:** Project success focus aligns individual response with team objectives
- **Format Specificity:** Detailed structure prevents information gaps that create additional email cycles

Category 5: Stakeholder Updates

Stakeholder update emails require strategic information presentation that builds confidence while maintaining transparency about challenges and progress.

Ready-to-Use Stakeholder Update Prompt:

```
None
Act as a competent project leader providing updates
to important stakeholders. Create a professional
update email based on the information in this
thread that keeps stakeholders informed while
demonstrating project control and progress. Present
information in a way that builds confidence in the
team's capabilities while being transparent about
any challenges. Structure as: 1) Brief executive
```

```
summary of current status, 2) Key accomplishments
or progress since last update, 3) Current
challenges and how they are being addressed, 4)
Upcoming milestones and timeline expectations, 5)
Any decisions or input needed from stakeholders.
Use    a    confident,    professional    tone    that
demonstrates competence and proactive management.
```

Implementation Process

Step 1: Identify Response Category

1. Read the email requiring response
2. Determine primary purpose: declining, following up, answering inquiry, coordinating, or updating
3. Select appropriate prompt template from the five categories above

Step 2: Execute Prompt in Outlook Copilot

1. Open the email thread in Microsoft Outlook
2. Click the Copilot icon in the email interface
3. Copy the selected prompt template
4. Paste into Copilot chat interface
5. Ensure the email thread is referenced or selected

Step 3: Review and Customize

1. Review generated response for accuracy and tone appropriateness
2. Add any specific details that require personalization
3. Verify all factual information and commitments
4. Adjust timeline or deadline references if needed

Step 4: Send with Confidence

1. Copy the refined response into your email composition window
2. Add appropriate subject line if needed
3. Send immediately, knowing the response is complete and professional

Quick Win Testing Sequence

Test 1: Polite Declination (3 minutes)

1. Find an email requesting something you need to decline
2. Use the Polite Declination prompt exactly as provided
3. Compare AI output time (30 seconds) vs. manual composition time (10+ minutes)
4. Note the diplomatic tone and relationship preservation elements

Test 2: Follow-Up Communication (3 minutes)

1. Identify an outstanding item requiring follow-up
2. Execute the Follow-Up Communication prompt
3. Observe how the response maintains persistence without pressure
4. Use the generated email to advance your project

Test 3: Client Response (5 minutes)

1. Select a client inquiry requiring comprehensive response
2. Apply the Client Inquiry Response prompt
3. Verify the response addresses both explicit and implicit concerns
4. Send the response and note improved client satisfaction

These systematic prompt templates eliminate the cognitive load of email composition while ensuring consistent professionalism across all your business communications. You now possess the technical capability to handle any email response scenario in under one minute while maintaining superior quality and strategic effectiveness.

2.2 The Instant Document Drafter

2.2.1 Generating First Drafts of Reports and Memos

The blank page represents one of the most paralyzing challenges in professional document creation. Staring at an empty Word document while facing a deadline creates cognitive pressure that inhibits creative thinking and strategic organization. Most professionals waste 20-30 minutes organizing their thoughts and structuring their approach before writing the first meaningful sentence.

The PTCF Framework eliminates blank page paralysis by providing systematic prompts that generate complete first drafts within minutes. You will master structured approaches that transform scattered ideas into professional documents with proper organization, tone, and completeness. These prompts serve as your strategic starting point, creating solid foundations that require only editing and refinement rather than complete composition from scratch.

Core Business Document Categories

Professional document creation falls into five essential categories, each requiring distinct prompt approaches:

- **Project Proposals:** Business case documents requesting approval or resources
- **Policy Memoranda:** Official communications announcing organizational changes
- **Status Reports:** Progress updates and performance summaries
- **Strategic Briefings:** Analysis documents supporting decision-making
- **Operational Procedures:** Step-by-step process documentation

Category 1: Project Proposals

Project proposals require persuasive structure that builds logical cases for resource allocation and organizational support. The PTCF Framework ensures comprehensive coverage of all decision-making factors.

Core Prompt Structure Analysis:

```
None
Persona: Act as a strategic business analyst with
project management expertise

Task: Create compelling proposal that demonstrates
value and feasibility

Context: Decision-makers need clear ROI
justification and implementation confidence

Format: Professional structure with executive
summary, business case, and action plan
```

Ready-to-Use Project Proposal Prompt:

```
None
Act as a strategic business analyst with project
management expertise. Create a comprehensive
one-page project proposal based on the following
information: [INSERT YOUR BULLET POINTS HERE].
Structure the proposal with these sections: 1)
Executive Summary (2-3 sentences stating the
project and primary benefit), 2) Business
Problem/Opportunity (brief description of what
needs to be addressed), 3) Proposed Solution (your
specific approach and key components), 4) Expected
```

```
Benefits (quantifiable outcomes and ROI where
possible), 5) Resource Requirements (timeline,
budget, and team needs), 6) Next Steps (immediate
actions needed for approval and launch). Use
professional, persuasive language that demonstrates
strategic thinking and practical implementation
planning. Keep the tone confident and
solution-focused while being realistic about
requirements and timelines.
```

Why This Prompt Works:

- **Persona Selection:** "Strategic business analyst with project management expertise" combines analytical credibility with practical implementation experience
- **Task Definition:** Clear directive to create compelling content ensures persuasive rather than merely informative output
- **Context Integration:** Decision-maker focus ensures all necessary evaluation criteria are addressed
- **Format Specification:** Six-section structure provides comprehensive coverage without overwhelming detail

Category 2: Policy Memoranda

Policy memoranda require authoritative tone combined with clear implementation guidance. These prompts generate official communications that establish organizational standards and expectations.

Ready-to-Use Policy Memorandum Prompt:

```
None
Act as a senior organizational leader communicating
important policy information. Create a formal
memorandum announcing the following policy change:
[INSERT POLICY DETAILS HERE]. Structure as a
professional memo with: 1) Header
(TO/FROM/DATE/SUBJECT format), 2) Purpose Statement
(why this policy is being implemented), 3) Policy
Details (specific rules, requirements, or changes),
4) Implementation Timeline (when changes take
effect and any transition period), 5) Impact on
Staff (how this affects daily operations and
responsibilities), 6) Support Resources (who to
contact for questions or assistance). Use
authoritative but approachable language that
demonstrates leadership while being helpful to
staff understanding. Ensure all critical
implementation details are included to prevent
confusion or non-compliance.
```

Category 3: Status Reports

Status reports require balanced presentation of progress, challenges, and forward-looking planning. These prompts ensure comprehensive coverage without overwhelming stakeholders with excessive detail.

Ready-to-Use Status Report Prompt:

```
None
Act as a competent project manager providing
stakeholder updates. Create a professional status
report covering the following information: [INSERT
STATUS DETAILS HERE]. Organize with these sections:
```

1) Executive Summary (current overall status in 2-3 sentences), 2) Accomplishments This Period (specific achievements and milestones completed), 3) Current Metrics (relevant data, percentages, or measurements), 4) Challenges and Issues (obstacles encountered and their impact), 5) Mitigation Actions (specific steps being taken to address problems), 6) Upcoming Priorities (next phase focus areas and key activities), 7) Resource Needs (any support required from stakeholders). Present information objectively while demonstrating proactive management and clear communication. Balance transparency about challenges with confidence in solutions and progress.

Category 4: Strategic Briefings

Strategic briefings require analytical depth combined with actionable recommendations. These prompts generate decision-support documents that synthesize complex information into executive-level insights.

Ready-to-Use Strategic Briefing Prompt:

```
None
```
Act as a senior business strategist preparing decision-support materials for leadership. Create an analytical briefing document based on this information: [INSERT ANALYSIS TOPICS/DATA HERE]. Structure with these components: 1) Situation Overview (current state and key factors), 2) Critical Analysis (examination of data, trends, or market conditions), 3) Strategic Options (2-3

potential approaches with pros/cons), 4) Recommended Action (preferred approach with clear rationale), 5) Implementation Considerations (timeline, resources, and potential obstacles), 6) Success Metrics (how to measure progress and outcomes). Use analytical language that demonstrates deep thinking while remaining accessible to non-technical executives. Focus on insights and implications rather than raw data presentation.

Category 5: Operational Procedures

Operational procedures require step-by-step clarity that eliminates ambiguity and ensures consistent execution. These prompts generate process documentation that supports organizational efficiency.

Ready-to-Use Operational Procedure Prompt:

None

Act as a process improvement specialist documenting organizational procedures. Create a clear operational procedure for the following process: [INSERT PROCESS DESCRIPTION HERE]. Format with these elements: 1) Purpose and Scope (what this procedure covers and why it exists), 2) Prerequisites (requirements or conditions before starting), 3) Step-by-Step Instructions (numbered sequence with specific actions), 4) Decision Points (where choices need to be made and criteria for decisions), 5) Quality Checkpoints (verification steps or approval requirements), 6) Troubleshooting (common problems and solutions), 7) Responsible Parties (roles and accountability for each major step). Write in clear, direct language using active voice and specific action verbs. Ensure each step is detailed enough for someone unfamiliar with the process to execute successfully.

Implementation Process

Step 1: Access Microsoft Word Copilot

1. Open Microsoft Word desktop application or web version
2. Create a new blank document
3. Look for the Copilot icon in the ribbon or sidebar
4. Click to activate the Copilot assistant panel

Step 2: Prepare Your Information

1. Gather all relevant details, bullet points, or data for your document
2. Organize key information in a simple list or outline format
3. Identify the document category from the five types above
4. Select the appropriate prompt template

Step 3: Execute Document Generation

1. Copy the selected prompt template exactly as written
2. Replace the placeholder text [INSERT YOUR INFORMATION HERE] with your specific content
3. Paste the complete prompt into Word Copilot
4. Allow 30-60 seconds for generation

Step 4: Review and Refine

1. Read through the generated first draft completely

2. Verify all key information is accurately included
3. Check that the tone and formality level match your needs
4. Make specific edits to personalize language and add details

Quick Win Testing Sequence

Test 1: Project Proposal (5 minutes)

1. Gather 4-5 bullet points about any project or initiative you need to propose
2. Use the Project Proposal prompt with your specific information
3. Compare AI generation time (2 minutes) vs. traditional drafting time (30+ minutes)
4. Note how the structure addresses all stakeholder concerns

Test 2: Policy Memo (5 minutes)

1. Think of any procedural change or announcement needed in your organization
2. Apply the Policy Memorandum prompt with your details
3. Observe how the format creates official, authoritative communication
4. Use the generated memo as a template for future policy communications

Test 3: Status Report (5 minutes)

1. Select any ongoing project or initiative requiring status updates
2. Execute the Status Report prompt with current progress information
3. Verify the balanced presentation of achievements, challenges, and next steps
4. Send the refined report to demonstrate proactive communication

These systematic document generation prompts eliminate the time-consuming ideation and organization phases of document creation. You now possess the technical capability to generate professional first drafts for any business document type within minutes, transforming your role from writer to strategic editor and allowing you to focus on refinement rather than creation from blank pages.

2.2.2 Rewriting and Refining Tone for Any Audience

Creating first drafts represents only half of professional document productivity. The refinement process, where you transform good content into excellent, audience-specific communication, traditionally consumes significant time and mental energy. Most professionals spend 40-60% of their document creation time editing, adjusting tone, and adapting content for different stakeholders.

The PTCF Framework transforms Microsoft Word Copilot into your expert editor, capable of systematic content refinement that maintains your core message while optimizing presentation for any audience. You will master structured prompts that modify existing text with surgical precision, eliminating the cognitive load of manual editing while ensuring professional excellence across all communications.

Core Text Refinement Categories

Professional content refinement serves six essential editing functions, each requiring distinct prompt approaches:

- **Conciseness Optimization:** Eliminating redundancy while preserving meaning
- **Tone Adjustment:** Modifying formality level for different audiences

- **Complexity Adaptation:** Simplifying or sophisticating language appropriately
- **Clarity Enhancement:** Improving readability and comprehension
- **Style Standardization:** Ensuring consistent voice across documents
- **Format Optimization:** Adapting structure for different communication channels

Category 1: Conciseness Optimization

Professional documents often contain unnecessary words, redundant phrases, and verbose explanations that dilute impact. Conciseness prompts eliminate inefficiencies while maintaining complete meaning and professional tone.

Core Prompt Structure Analysis:

```
None
Persona: Act as a professional editor specializing in business communication

Task: Reduce word count while preserving all essential meaning and impact

Context: Busy professionals need clear, direct communication without unnecessary length

Format: Maintain original structure while eliminating redundancy and wordiness
```

Ready-to-Use Conciseness Prompt:

None

Act as a professional editor specializing in business communication. Rewrite the following text to be more concise while preserving all essential meaning, key details, and professional tone. Eliminate redundant phrases, unnecessary qualifiers, and verbose explanations. Focus on direct, clear language that communicates the same information in fewer words. Maintain the original structure and formatting, but ensure every word serves a purpose. Target a 25-40% reduction in length without losing any critical information or changing the core message.

[PASTE YOUR TEXT HERE]

Why This Prompt Works:

- **Persona Precision:** "Professional editor specializing in business communication" ensures appropriate expertise level
- **Task Specification:** Clear directive with quantifiable outcome (25-40% reduction) provides measurable guidance
- **Context Integration:** Acknowledges busy professional audience requiring efficiency
- **Format Preservation:** Maintains document structure while optimizing content

Category 2: Tone Adjustment for Executive Audiences

Executive communications require elevated formality, strategic focus, and confident presentation. These prompts transform operational-level content into C-suite appropriate messaging.

Ready-to-Use Executive Tone Adjustment Prompt:

```
None
Act as a senior executive communications
specialist. Rewrite the following text to be
appropriate for an executive audience, including
C-level leaders and board members. Adjust the tone
to be more formal, strategic, and authoritative
while maintaining all factual content. Use
executive-level language that demonstrates
strategic thinking, focuses on business impact and
outcomes, and eliminates operational details unless
critical for decision-making. Ensure the writing
conveys confidence and competence appropriate for
senior leadership review.


[PASTE YOUR TEXT HERE]
```

Category 3: Technical Content Simplification

Technical content often requires adaptation for non-technical stakeholders who need to understand concepts without specialized knowledge. These prompts maintain accuracy while improving accessibility.

Ready-to-Use Technical Simplification Prompt:

```
None
Act as a technical communication expert who
specializes in making complex information
accessible. Rewrite the following technical content
for a non-technical business audience. Replace
jargon with plain language, explain technical
```

concepts using business-relevant analogies, and focus on practical implications rather than technical details. Maintain accuracy while ensuring the content is understandable to someone without specialized technical knowledge. Structure explanations to show how technical aspects relate to business outcomes and decision-making.

[PASTE YOUR TEXT HERE]

Category 4: Clarity Enhancement

Clarity enhancement improves readability, logical flow, and comprehension without changing fundamental content or tone. These prompts address structural and linguistic barriers to understanding.

Ready-to-Use Clarity Enhancement Prompt:

None

Act as an experienced business writing coach focused on clarity and readability. Rewrite the following text to improve clarity and comprehension while maintaining the original tone and message. Break down complex sentences, improve logical flow between ideas, and ensure each paragraph has a clear focus. Use active voice where appropriate, eliminate ambiguous references, and ensure transitions between concepts are smooth and logical. The goal is to make the content easier to read and understand without changing the core meaning or professional tone.

[PASTE YOUR TEXT HERE]

Category 5: Style Standardization

Style standardization ensures consistent voice, formatting, and presentation across organizational communications. These prompts align content with established communication standards.

Ready-to-Use Style Standardization Prompt:

```
None
Act as a corporate communications standards specialist. Rewrite the following text to align with professional business communication standards. Ensure consistent use of active voice, parallel structure in lists, appropriate paragraph length (3-5 sentences), and professional language throughout. Standardize formatting for consistency, use clear headings where appropriate, and ensure the writing style matches formal business communication expectations. Maintain the original message and tone while improving overall professionalism and consistency.
```

[PASTE YOUR TEXT HERE]

Category 6: Format Optimization for Different Channels

Different communication channels require distinct formatting and presentation approaches. These prompts adapt content structure for optimal effectiveness across platforms.

Ready-to-Use Email Format Optimization Prompt:

```
None
Act as a digital communication specialist. Rewrite
the following content to be optimized for email
communication. Structure with a clear
subject-appropriate opening, scannable body
paragraphs with key information highlighted, and a
specific call-to-action or next steps section.
Ensure the content is mobile-friendly with shorter
paragraphs, bullet points for complex information,
and clear section breaks. Maintain professional
tone while adapting structure for busy
professionals reading on various devices.


[PASTE YOUR TEXT HERE]
```

Implementation Process

Step 1: Access Microsoft Word Copilot

1. Open your existing document in Microsoft Word
2. Select the text section requiring refinement
3. Click the Copilot icon in the Word ribbon or sidebar
4. Activate the AI assistant panel

Step 2: Identify Refinement Objective

1. Determine primary goal: conciseness, tone adjustment, simplification, clarity, standardization, or format optimization

2. Consider your target audience and communication purpose
3. Select appropriate prompt template from the six categories above

Step 3: Execute Refinement Process

1. Copy the selected prompt template exactly as written
2. Paste your target text in the designated placeholder area
3. Submit the complete prompt to Word Copilot
4. Allow 30-45 seconds for processing

Step 4: Review and Apply Changes

1. Compare original text with AI-generated refinement
2. Verify that core meaning and critical details are preserved
3. Make any necessary minor adjustments for your specific context
4. Replace original text with refined version

Advanced Refinement Techniques

Sequential Refinement Process: For complex documents requiring multiple improvements, apply refinements sequentially:

1. **First Pass:** Conciseness optimization to eliminate unnecessary length
2. **Second Pass:** Tone adjustment for target audience
3. **Third Pass:** Clarity enhancement for final polish
4. **Final Review:** Style standardization for consistency

Comparative Refinement Analysis: Use this prompt to evaluate multiple refinement approaches:

```
None
Act as a communications consultant comparing
different versions of the same content. I will
provide you with an original text and two refined
```

versions. Analyze the strengths and weaknesses of each version in terms of clarity, conciseness, tone appropriateness, and overall effectiveness. Recommend which version best serves the intended purpose and suggest any additional improvements.

Original Text: [PASTE ORIGINAL]

Version A: [PASTE FIRST REFINEMENT]

Version B: [PASTE SECOND REFINEMENT]

Quick Win Testing Protocol

Test 1: Conciseness Optimization (5 minutes)

1. Select a lengthy paragraph from any existing document
2. Apply the Conciseness Prompt exactly as provided
3. Compare word count reduction and clarity improvement
4. Note how essential meaning remains intact

Test 2: Executive Tone Adjustment (5 minutes)

1. Choose operational-level content requiring executive presentation
2. Execute the Executive Tone Adjustment Prompt
3. Observe language elevation and strategic positioning
4. Use refined content for actual executive communication

Test 3: Technical Simplification (5 minutes)

1. Find technical content requiring broader audience understanding
2. Apply the Technical Simplification Prompt

3. Verify accuracy maintenance while improving accessibility
4. Test comprehension with non-technical colleagues

These systematic refinement prompts transform Microsoft Word Copilot into your expert editing partner, enabling professional-quality content adaptation for any audience or purpose. You now possess the technical capability to refine any document within minutes while maintaining superior quality standards and strategic communication effectiveness.

3. Master Your Meetings and Collaboration

You have successfully transformed your communication workflow using the PTCF Framework. Email threads that once consumed hours now yield actionable summaries in minutes. Documents that previously required lengthy composition sessions now emerge as polished drafts within moments. Your inbox operates at zero, and your document creation process flows with systematic efficiency.

These communication victories, however significant, represent only the foundation of your productivity transformation. The next frontier demands mastery over the most time-consuming and mentally draining aspect of modern professional life: meetings and collaborative work.

The Meeting Epidemic

Meeting overload represents the single greatest threat to professional productivity in today's workplace. The average knowledge worker spends 37% of their time in meetings, attending an average of 62 meetings per month. This translates to 23 hours weekly dedicated to collaborative discussions, presentations, and coordination sessions.

The productivity cost extends far beyond raw time investment. Meetings fragment deep work sessions, create cognitive switching penalties, and generate cascading administrative overhead that consumes additional hours for preparation, follow-up, and coordination activities. I have observed professionals spend 3-4 hours preparing for a single one-hour strategic presentation, then require another 2 hours processing action items and distributing follow-up communications.

Meeting inefficiency compounds exponentially across organizations. Consider the true cost of a typical weekly team meeting involving eight professionals earning average corporate salaries. The direct time cost exceeds $2,000 weekly, translating to over $100,000 annually for a single recurring meeting. When preparation time, follow-up activities, and opportunity costs are included, the actual investment approaches $300,000 per year for one team's weekly coordination.

The Collaboration Productivity Paradox

Modern collaboration tools promise enhanced teamwork and communication efficiency, yet most professionals report feeling more overwhelmed by collaborative demands than ever before. Microsoft Teams generates an average of 45 notifications per user daily. Calendar applications show meeting density increasing 13% annually across corporate environments. Presentation creation consumes 6-8 hours weekly for management-level professionals.

The paradox emerges because collaboration tools focus on connection rather than systematic efficiency. Platforms excel at facilitating communication but provide no framework for optimizing the quality, preparation, or outcomes of collaborative interactions. Most professionals approach meetings with the same reactive mindset they bring to email management: responding to requests, attending without strategic preparation, and processing outcomes manually.

This reactive approach creates collaborative debt similar to the digital debt addressed in your communication transformation. Meeting requests accumulate without strategic evaluation. Preparation happens frantically in the minutes before sessions begin. Action items emerge from discussions but disappear into email chaos or forgotten notebook pages. Follow-up communications drain additional time while providing minimal value.

The Meeting Mastery Opportunity

The PTCF Framework transforms meeting and collaboration challenges into systematic productivity advantages. Every aspect of collaborative work, from initial preparation through final follow-up, can be optimized using structured prompts that eliminate manual inefficiencies while enhancing professional impact.

Meeting preparation, traditionally consuming hours of scattered research and agenda creation, becomes a 10-minute systematic process. Complex presentation development, typically requiring days of content organization and slide creation, transforms into streamlined workflows that generate professional results in under an hour. Post-meeting follow-up, often delayed or incomplete due to competing priorities, executes automatically with precision and completeness.

The strategic advantage emerges from consistent application of systematic approaches rather than reliance on individual meeting performance or spontaneous preparation quality. Your collaborative effectiveness becomes predictable and scalable, independent of workload pressures or competing deadlines.

System 1: The Automated Meeting Assistant

The Automated Meeting Assistant leverages Microsoft Teams Copilot to manage the complete meeting lifecycle through systematic prompt sequences. This system addresses three critical phases of collaborative interaction: preparation, execution, and follow-up.

Pre-Meeting Intelligence Generation Traditional meeting preparation relies on manual research, scattered document review, and individual memory of previous discussions. The Automated Meeting Assistant transforms preparation into systematic intelligence gathering that synthesizes historical context, identifies key decision points, and generates comprehensive briefing materials.

You will master prompts that analyze Teams channel history to extract relevant background information, synthesize document attachments into actionable briefings, and generate agenda frameworks tailored to specific meeting types. These preparation prompts eliminate the scattered research phase while ensuring comprehensive coverage of all relevant context.

Real-Time Meeting Enhancement During meetings, the system leverages live transcription capabilities to capture decisions, identify action items, and track unresolved questions without manual note-taking effort. You will learn to structure meetings for optimal AI capture while maintaining natural discussion flow.

Automated Follow-Up Execution Post-meeting processing transforms from time-intensive manual effort into systematic extraction and distribution of outcomes. The system generates action item summaries, decision documentation, and follow-up communication templates that ensure nothing falls through administrative cracks.

System 2: The Presentation Power-Up

The Presentation Power-Up applies PTCF Framework principles to Microsoft PowerPoint Copilot, transforming presentation creation from lengthy design sessions into rapid content development and professional formatting processes.

Rapid Content Structure Generation Instead of starting with blank presentations and manually organizing ideas, you will generate comprehensive presentation outlines from existing documents, meeting notes, or strategic briefings. The system creates logical flow, identifies key messaging hierarchies, and suggests optimal slide sequences for maximum audience impact.

Cross-Application Content Integration The Presentation Power-Up demonstrates advanced PTCF Framework application by coordinating content across multiple Microsoft 365 applications. Word documents become presentation foundations. Excel data transforms into compelling visual narratives. Teams discussion summaries evolve into stakeholder briefing materials.

Speaker Enhancement Support Beyond slide creation, the system generates speaker notes, talking point sequences, and audience-specific messaging adaptations that enhance delivery confidence and impact. You will master prompts that adapt technical content for executive audiences, create compelling narratives from analytical data, and develop persuasive arguments from strategic documentation.

The Collaborative Transformation Promise

This chapter represents your transition from individual productivity optimization to collaborative leadership. The skills you will master position you as the professional who comes prepared to every meeting, delivers compelling presentations consistently, and ensures collaborative outcomes achieve systematic follow-through.

Your meeting preparation time will reduce from hours to minutes while improving comprehensive coverage of relevant context. Presentation creation will accelerate from days to hours while maintaining professional design standards and compelling content organization. Post-meeting follow-up will execute with completeness and precision, ensuring collaborative decisions translate into organizational progress.

More significantly, you will model systematic collaborative excellence for your teams and stakeholders. Your preparation quality, presentation impact, and follow-up reliability will distinguish your professional contributions while encouraging organizational adoption of similar systematic approaches.

Chapter Implementation Framework

The two systems in this chapter build directly upon your existing PTCF Framework mastery. Every meeting prompt applies the Persona, Task, Context, Format structure you have internalized through communication automation. The complexity increases through coordination across multiple applications and collaborative scenarios, but the underlying systematic approach remains consistent.

You will progress from individual meeting optimization to complex presentation development, then to integrated workflows that coordinate multiple collaborative interactions simultaneously. Each system provides immediate productivity benefits while building capabilities for advanced collaborative scenarios.

The transformation you will achieve extends your professional impact from individual efficiency to collaborative leadership, positioning you as the strategist who leverages AI augmentation to elevate team productivity and organizational outcomes.

3.1 THE AUTOMATED MEETING ASSISTANT

3.1.1 GENERATING PRE-MEETING BRIEFINGS AND AGENDAS

Walking into meetings unprepared represents one of the most damaging professional habits in collaborative work environments. Poorly prepared participants waste collective time, miss strategic opportunities, and undermine their credibility with colleagues and stakeholders. The average professional spends only 8 minutes preparing for meetings, yet expects productive outcomes from complex discussions requiring comprehensive background knowledge.

Traditional meeting preparation involves scattered research across multiple platforms: reviewing email threads, scanning shared documents, checking previous meeting notes, and attempting to synthesize fragmented information into coherent understanding. This manual approach consumes significant time while producing incomplete context, leaving you reactive rather than strategic in collaborative discussions.

Microsoft Teams Copilot transforms meeting preparation from time-intensive research into systematic intelligence gathering that delivers comprehensive briefings within minutes. You will master systematic prompts that analyze channel history, synthesize document context, and generate strategic agendas that position you as the prepared professional who drives meeting effectiveness.

Core Pre-Meeting Intelligence Categories

Effective meeting preparation requires systematic information synthesis across five critical areas:

- **Historical Context Analysis:** Understanding previous discussions, decisions, and unresolved issues
- **Document Intelligence Extraction:** Synthesizing key information from relevant attachments and shared files

- **Participant Background Research:** Identifying stakeholder priorities and relevant expertise areas
- **Strategic Agenda Development:** Creating structured discussion frameworks that maximize meeting productivity
- **Decision Point Identification:** Highlighting critical choices requiring meeting resolution

Category 1: Historical Context Analysis

Historical context analysis synthesizes previous channel discussions, email threads, and meeting outcomes to provide comprehensive background understanding. These prompts eliminate manual scrolling and searching through communication history.

Ready-to-Use Channel History Analysis Prompt:

```
None
Act as a meeting preparation specialist. Analyze
the recent discussion history in this Microsoft
Teams channel over the past [INSERT TIME FRAME: 2
weeks, 1 month, etc.] to prepare me for our
upcoming [INSERT MEETING TYPE: weekly sync, project
review, strategic planning session]. Create a
comprehensive briefing that includes: 1) Key
Discussion Themes (main topics and recurring
concerns), 2) Decisions Made (any choices or
commitments established), 3) Outstanding Issues
(unresolved problems or questions), 4) Action Items
Status (completed tasks and pending activities), 5)
Participant Contributions (who has been most active
and their focus areas). Focus on information
directly relevant to our upcoming meeting agenda
and highlight any urgent items requiring immediate
attention.
```

Why This Prompt Works:

- **Persona Specification:** "Meeting preparation specialist" ensures focused, professional analysis rather than casual summarization
- **Time Frame Customization:** Allows adjustment for different meeting cadences and context requirements
- **Structured Output:** Five distinct categories ensure comprehensive coverage without overwhelming detail
- **Relevance Filter:** Focuses analysis on meeting-appropriate information rather than casual conversation

Category 2: Document Intelligence Extraction

Document intelligence extraction synthesizes information from attachments, shared files, and linked resources to provide comprehensive content understanding without manual document review.

Ready-to-Use Document Analysis Prompt:

```
None
Act as a strategic business analyst preparing
executive briefings. Analyze the attached documents
[or: documents shared in this channel] to create a
meeting preparation summary for our upcoming
[INSERT MEETING TYPE]. Structure your analysis as:
1) Executive Summary (key findings and main themes
in 2-3 sentences), 2) Critical Information (most
important facts, figures, or decisions for meeting
discussion), 3) Strategic Implications (how this
information affects our project/business
objectives), 4) Discussion Points (specific
questions or topics this information suggests for
meeting agenda), 5) Action Requirements (any
immediate steps or decisions this information
indicates we need to address). Focus on insights
```

that will enable productive strategic discussion rather than detailed technical analysis.

Category 3: Strategic Agenda Development

Strategic agenda development creates structured discussion frameworks that maximize meeting productivity and ensure comprehensive coverage of critical topics.

Ready-to-Use Agenda Generation Prompt:

```
None
Act as an expert meeting facilitator creating
strategic agendas. Generate a comprehensive agenda
for our [INSERT MEETING TYPE: project kick-off,
quarterly review, team planning session] based on
the following context: [INSERT RELEVANT
INFORMATION: project goals, team priorities, key
challenges, etc.]. Structure the agenda with: 1)
Meeting Objectives (specific outcomes we need to
achieve), 2) Time-Allocated Discussion Items
(topics with suggested duration), 3) Decision
Points (choices requiring resolution during this
meeting), 4) Information Sharing (updates or
reports needed from participants), 5) Action
Planning (next steps and responsibility
assignments). Design for a [INSERT DURATION]
meeting that keeps discussion focused and achieves
concrete results. Include suggested time
allocations for each agenda item.
```

Category 4: Participant Intelligence Synthesis

Participant intelligence synthesis provides background context on meeting attendees, their expertise areas, and relevant priorities to facilitate more effective collaboration.

Ready-to-Use Participant Background Prompt:

```
None
Act as a collaboration strategist preparing for
stakeholder meetings. Based on the participants
invited to this meeting [INSERT PARTICIPANT LIST
OR: attendees shown in the meeting invitation],
provide a strategic briefing that includes: 1)
Expertise Areas (each person's relevant knowledge
and experience), 2) Project Involvement (their role
and responsibilities in current initiatives), 3)
Decision Authority (their influence over choices we
need to make), 4) Communication Preferences (how
they typically engage in collaborative
discussions), 5) Strategic Priorities (their likely
concerns and objectives for this meeting). Use
information from recent channel discussions, shared
documents, and previous meeting participation to
build comprehensive participant profiles. Focus on
insights that will help me facilitate more
effective collaboration.
```

Category 5: Meeting Context Integration

Meeting context integration combines historical discussions, document analysis, and participant intelligence into unified briefing materials that provide complete meeting preparation.

Ready-to-Use Comprehensive Meeting Briefing Prompt:

```
None
Act as a senior executive assistant preparing
comprehensive meeting briefings. Create a complete
pre-meeting intelligence summary for our upcoming
[INSERT MEETING TYPE] scheduled for [INSERT
DATE/TIME]. Synthesize information from: recent
channel discussions, shared documents, participant
backgrounds, and previous meeting outcomes to
provide: 1) Meeting Context (why this meeting is
happening and its strategic importance), 2)
Background Intelligence (key information all
participants should know), 3) Critical Discussion
Areas (topics requiring focused attention), 4)
Potential Challenges (issues that might complicate
discussion or decision-making), 5) Success Metrics
(how to measure if this meeting achieves its
objectives), 6) Preparation Recommendations (what
participants should review or prepare before
attending). Structure as an executive-level
briefing that enables strategic rather than
reactive meeting participation.
```

Implementation Workflow

Step 1: Access Microsoft Teams Copilot

1. Open Microsoft Teams desktop application or web version
2. Navigate to the relevant channel or chat for your upcoming meeting
3. Click the Copilot icon in the Teams interface (typically in the compose area or toolbar)
4. Ensure you have access to the channel history and relevant documents

Step 2: Execute Historical Analysis

1. Copy the Channel History Analysis prompt template
2. Customize the time frame and meeting type for your specific context
3. Submit the prompt to Teams Copilot
4. Review generated analysis for key discussion themes and outstanding issues

Step 3: Process Document Intelligence

1. Apply the Document Analysis prompt to any meeting-relevant files
2. Focus on attachments, shared documents, or linked resources
3. Extract strategic implications and discussion points
4. Identify information requiring meeting decisions or actions

Step 4: Generate Strategic Agenda

1. Use the Agenda Generation prompt with your specific meeting parameters
2. Include context from historical analysis and document review
3. Ensure time allocations match your scheduled meeting duration
4. Distribute agenda to participants for advance review

Step 5: Complete Preparation Synthesis

1. Execute the Comprehensive Meeting Briefing prompt for final preparation
2. Combine insights from all previous analysis steps
3. Create executive summary for quick pre-meeting review
4. Identify key talking points and strategic priorities

Advanced Meeting Preparation Techniques

Sequential Preparation Process: For high-stakes meetings, apply prompts sequentially to build comprehensive understanding:

1. **Week Before:** Execute Historical Context Analysis to understand background
2. **3 Days Before:** Process Document Intelligence for detailed content knowledge
3. **Day Before:** Generate Strategic Agenda and distribute to participants
4. **Morning Of:** Create Comprehensive Meeting Briefing for final preparation

Cross-Meeting Intelligence Building: Use this prompt to connect insights across related meetings:

```
None
Act as a strategic project coordinator tracking meeting outcomes across multiple sessions. Analyze the progression of decisions, action items, and discussion themes from our previous [INSERT NUMBER] meetings on [INSERT TOPIC/PROJECT] to identify: 1) Decision Evolution (how choices have developed over time), 2) Recurring Challenges (issues that keep arising), 3) Progress Indicators (measurable advancement toward objectives), 4) Stakeholder Alignment (areas of agreement and persistent disagreements), 5) Strategic Momentum (whether we are accelerating or losing focus). Use this analysis to recommend focus areas for our upcoming meeting that will maximize strategic progress.
```

Quick Win Testing Protocol

Test 1: Channel History Analysis (5 minutes)

1. Select a Teams channel with recent discussion activity
2. Apply the Channel History Analysis prompt for the past two weeks

3. Compare AI-generated insights with your manual memory of discussions
4. Note how systematic analysis reveals missed context and connections

Test 2: Document-Based Agenda Creation (5 minutes)

1. Choose an upcoming meeting with relevant shared documents
2. Execute the Agenda Generation prompt using document context
3. Compare generated agenda with your typical preparation approach
4. Use structured agenda for actual meeting and observe improved discussion quality

Test 3: Comprehensive Meeting Briefing (10 minutes)

1. Apply the full preparation workflow for an important upcoming meeting
2. Measure total preparation time compared to manual research approach
3. Assess meeting performance improvement through systematic preparation
4. Document effectiveness for future high-stakes meeting preparation

These systematic pre-meeting preparation prompts transform your collaborative effectiveness from reactive participation to strategic leadership. You now possess the technical capability to enter every meeting with comprehensive context, strategic agenda control, and thorough participant understanding that positions you as the prepared professional driving meeting productivity and outcomes.

3.1.2 Capturing Action Items and Decisions from Transcripts

Post-meeting follow-up represents the most neglected yet critical phase of collaborative productivity. Surveys indicate that 67% of professionals admit to forgetting meeting commitments within 24 hours, while 43% of action items assigned during meetings never receive follow-up tracking. This systematic failure transforms productive discussions into wasted time, erodes team accountability, and creates recurring cycles of unresolved issues.

Manual transcript analysis consumes 15-30 minutes per hour of meeting content. Most professionals resort to hasty note-taking during discussions, missing crucial details while attempting to capture decisions and commitments. The resulting incomplete action item lists create confusion about responsibilities, deadlines, and follow-up requirements that undermine project momentum.

Microsoft Teams Copilot transforms post-meeting processing from memory-dependent manual work into systematic analysis that extracts complete decision records, comprehensive action item lists, and strategic insight summaries. You will master structured prompts that process meeting transcripts with surgical precision, ensuring nothing falls through administrative cracks while positioning you as the collaborative professional who delivers consistent follow-through.

Core Post-Meeting Analysis Categories

Effective transcript analysis requires systematic extraction across six critical information types:

- **Action Item Identification:** Specific tasks, responsibilities, and deadline commitments
- **Decision Documentation:** Choices made, alternatives considered, and rationale provided
- **Issue Resolution Tracking:** Problems solved and outstanding concerns requiring attention

- **Stakeholder Commitment Recording:** Individual promises, agreements, and accountability assignments
- **Follow-Up Requirement Analysis:** Next meetings, check-ins, and progress review schedules
- **Strategic Context Synthesis:** Key themes, priorities, and project direction insights

Category 1: Action Item Identification and Organization

Action item identification systematically extracts all task assignments, responsibility allocations, and deadline commitments from meeting discussions. These prompts eliminate the guesswork about who committed to what actions by when.

Ready-to-Use Action Item Extraction Prompt:

```
None
Act as a project coordination specialist focused on
accountability and follow-through. Analyze the
meeting transcript to create a comprehensive action
item summary organized as a detailed table.
Structure with these columns: 1) Action Item
(specific task or deliverable described), 2)
Assigned Owner (person responsible for completion),
3) Deadline/Timeline (specific date or timeframe
mentioned), 4) Dependencies (other people,
resources, or tasks required), 5) Success Criteria
(how completion will be measured or verified).
Include every commitment made during the
discussion, regardless of how informally it was
stated. If any information is unclear or missing
from the transcript, note "To be clarified" in the
appropriate field. Focus on actionable tasks that
require follow-up rather than general discussion
points.
```

Why This Prompt Works:

- **Persona Precision:** "Project coordination specialist focused on accountability" ensures systematic rather than casual analysis
- **Table Structure:** Five-column format captures all essential task management information
- **Comprehensiveness Directive:** "Include every commitment" prevents overlooking informal assignments
- **Clarity Handling:** "To be clarified" notation addresses incomplete information professionally

Category 2: Decision Documentation and Rationale Capture

Decision documentation captures choices made during meetings along with supporting rationale and alternative considerations. These prompts create permanent records that prevent future confusion about why specific directions were chosen.

Ready-to-Use Decision Documentation Prompt:

```
Act as a strategic business analyst documenting executive decisions. Review the meeting transcript to identify and document all decisions made during the discussion. Create a comprehensive decision log with: 1) Decision Statement (clear description of what was decided), 2) Decision Owner (person with authority who made the final choice), 3) Supporting Rationale (reasons and logic provided for this decision), 4) Alternatives Considered (other options discussed and why they were rejected), 5) Implementation Impact (how this decision affects current projects or processes), 6) Review Timeline (when this decision should be revisited or evaluated). Focus on choices that will guide future actions rather than minor procedural agreements.
```

Include both explicit decisions and implied agreements that emerged from the discussion.

Category 3: Issue Resolution and Outstanding Concern Analysis

Issue resolution analysis distinguishes between problems solved during meetings and concerns requiring additional attention. These prompts ensure unresolved issues receive proper tracking and follow-up prioritization.

Ready-to-Use Issue Resolution Tracking Prompt:

```
None
Act as a business operations analyst tracking issue
resolution and risk management. Examine the meeting
transcript to categorize all problems, concerns,
and challenges discussed. Organize findings into
two sections: 1) RESOLVED ISSUES - problems that
received complete solutions during the meeting with
implementation details, and 2) OUTSTANDING CONCERNS
- unresolved problems requiring additional
attention. For each outstanding concern, provide:
Problem Description, Potential Impact, Proposed
Next Steps, Responsible Party, and Urgency Level
(High/Medium/Low). Include any risks, obstacles, or
challenges mentioned that could affect project
success. Focus on substantive issues that require
management attention rather than minor technical
clarifications.
```

Category 4: Stakeholder Commitment and Agreement Recording

Stakeholder commitment recording captures individual promises, resource allocations, and collaborative agreements made during meetings. These prompts create accountability frameworks that strengthen team coordination.

Ready-to-Use Commitment Recording Prompt:

```
None
Act as a team coordination specialist focused on
accountability and resource management. Analyze the
meeting transcript to identify all commitments,
promises, and resource allocations made by
individual participants. Create a commitment
summary organized by person with: 1) Participant
Name, 2) Specific Commitments Made (tasks,
resources, or support promised), 3) Timeline for
Delivery, 4) Dependencies on Others (what they need
from teammates), 5) Resource Requirements (budget,
tools, or access needed). Include informal
agreements and verbal commitments alongside formal
task assignments. Note any conditions or
contingencies attached to commitments. Focus on
creating clear accountability records that prevent
misunderstandings about individual
responsibilities.
```

Category 5: Follow-Up Requirement and Schedule Analysis

Follow-up requirement analysis identifies all future meeting needs, check-in schedules, and progress review timelines established during discussions. These prompts ensure continuous project momentum through systematic scheduling.

Ready-to-Use Follow-Up Planning Prompt:

```
None
Act as a meeting coordination specialist managing
project schedules and follow-up requirements.
Review the meeting transcript to identify all
future meeting needs, check-ins, and follow-up
activities mentioned. Create a follow-up schedule
with: 1) Follow-Up Type (progress check, decision
meeting, review session, etc.), 2) Proposed
Timeline (when this should occur), 3) Required
Participants (who needs to attend), 4) Purpose and
Agenda (what needs to be accomplished), 5)
Prerequisites (work that must be completed before
the meeting), 6) Expected Outcomes (decisions or
deliverables expected). Include both scheduled
meetings and suggested check-ins. Prioritize
follow-ups based on project timeline and dependency
requirements.
```

Category 6: Strategic Context and Theme Synthesis

Strategic context synthesis extracts high-level themes, priorities, and directional insights that inform broader project understanding and stakeholder communication.

Ready-to-Use Strategic Context Prompt:

```
None
Act as a strategic communication consultant
preparing executive briefings. Analyze the meeting
transcript to identify overarching themes,
strategic priorities, and key insights that emerged
from the discussion. Create a strategic context
summary with: 1) Primary Themes (main topics and
```

focus areas), 2) Strategic Priorities (most important objectives and goals discussed), 3) Stakeholder Perspectives (different viewpoints or concerns expressed), 4) Resource Implications (budget, staffing, or capability needs identified), 5) Risk Factors (potential challenges or obstacles mentioned), 6) Success Indicators (metrics or milestones for measuring progress). Focus on strategic-level insights rather than tactical details. Structure as an executive summary suitable for senior stakeholder briefing.

Implementation Workflow

Step 1: Access Teams Meeting Transcript

1. Open Microsoft Teams and navigate to your completed meeting
2. Click on the meeting in your Teams calendar or chat history
3. Locate the "Transcript" tab or section within the meeting details
4. Verify the transcript is complete and accurate for analysis

Step 2: Execute Core Analysis Sequence

1. **Action Items First:** Apply the Action Item Extraction prompt to capture all task assignments
2. **Decision Documentation:** Use Decision Documentation prompt to record choices made
3. **Issue Resolution:** Execute Issue Resolution Tracking prompt for problem analysis
4. **Commitment Recording:** Apply Commitment Recording prompt for accountability tracking

Step 3: Generate Follow-Up Materials

1. Use Follow-Up Planning prompt to schedule future interactions
2. Apply Strategic Context prompt for executive summary creation
3. Combine outputs into comprehensive meeting summary document
4. Distribute summary to all participants for confirmation and clarity

Step 4: Create Action Tracking System

1. Transfer action items to your preferred project management tool
2. Set calendar reminders for deadline tracking and progress check-ins
3. Schedule follow-up meetings identified in the analysis
4. Establish accountability check-in processes for commitment tracking

Advanced Transcript Analysis Techniques

Sequential Analysis Process: For complex strategic meetings, apply prompts in systematic sequence to build comprehensive understanding:

1. **Strategic Context First:** Understand overall themes and priorities
2. **Decision Documentation:** Capture choices and rationale
3. **Action Item Extraction:** Identify specific tasks and responsibilities
4. **Follow-Up Planning:** Schedule continuation activities

Cross-Meeting Pattern Analysis: Use this prompt to identify recurring themes across multiple meetings:

```
None
Act as a strategic project analyst tracking
patterns across multiple meeting sessions. Compare
the issues, decisions, and action items from the
past [INSERT NUMBER] meetings on [INSERT
PROJECT/TOPIC] to identify: 1) Recurring Challenges
(problems that keep appearing), 2) Progress
Patterns (areas showing consistent advancement or
stagnation), 3) Decision Evolution (how choices
have changed over time), 4) Resource Constraint
Themes (persistent budget, staffing, or capability
limitations), 5) Stakeholder Alignment Trends
(areas of increasing agreement or persistent
disagreement). Use this analysis to recommend focus
areas for improving meeting effectiveness and
project outcomes.
```

Quick Win Testing Protocol

Test 1: Action Item Extraction (5 minutes)

1. Select a recent meeting with multiple task assignments
2. Apply the Action Item Extraction prompt to the transcript
3. Compare AI-generated action items with your manual notes
4. Note how systematic extraction reveals missed commitments and responsibilities

Test 2: Decision Documentation (5 minutes)

1. Choose a meeting where important choices were made
2. Execute the Decision Documentation prompt
3. Assess how comprehensive decision recording improves future reference
4. Use documented rationale for stakeholder communication

Test 3: Complete Follow-Up Workflow (10 minutes)

1. Apply the full transcript analysis sequence to a strategic meeting
2. Generate comprehensive follow-up summary using all six prompt categories
3. Measure time savings compared to manual summary creation
4. Distribute systematic summary and observe improved team alignment and accountability

These systematic transcript analysis prompts transform post-meeting processing from incomplete manual effort into comprehensive intelligence extraction that ensures nothing falls through collaborative cracks. You now possess the technical capability to capture every decision, track all commitments, and create accountability systems that position you as the collaborative professional who delivers consistent follow-through and strategic project coordination.

3.2 THE PRESENTATION POWER-UP

3.2.1 CREATING PRESENTATION OUTLINES FROM DOCUMENTS

Presentation creation represents one of the most time-intensive collaborative activities in modern professional environments. The average business presentation requires 6-8 hours of development time: 2-3 hours organizing content structure, 2-3 hours creating slide layouts, and 2-3 hours refining messaging and visual design. This manual process creates productivity bottlenecks that delay project timelines and consume strategic thinking capacity.

Traditional presentation development begins with the dreaded blank PowerPoint template, forcing you to manually extract key points from source documents, organize logical flow, and structure compelling narratives from scattered information. Most professionals resort to copying and pasting text blocks from reports, then spending hours reformatting content into presentation-appropriate messaging.

Microsoft PowerPoint Copilot transforms presentation creation from lengthy manual construction into systematic document-to-presentation workflows that generate structured outlines, logical slide sequences, and audience-appropriate messaging within minutes. You will master cross-application prompts that convert existing Word documents, Excel reports, and strategic briefings into compelling presentation frameworks ready for refinement and delivery.

Core Document-to-Presentation Categories

Effective presentation outline generation requires systematic approaches across five essential document types:

- **Strategic Document Conversion:** Transforming business plans, reports, and strategic briefings into executive presentations

- **Data Report Visualization:** Converting analytical documents and Excel summaries into data-driven presentations
- **Process Documentation Presentation:** Adapting procedural documents and training materials into instructional slide sequences
- **Proposal and Pitch Development:** Creating persuasive presentations from project proposals and business case documents
- **Update and Review Formatting:** Structuring status reports and progress summaries into stakeholder presentation formats

Category 1: Strategic Document Conversion

Strategic document conversion transforms comprehensive business documents into executive-level presentations that distill complex information into decision-focused slide sequences.

Ready-to-Use Strategic Document Conversion Prompt:

```
None
Act as an executive presentation specialist
creating strategic briefings for senior leadership.
Create a comprehensive presentation outline based
on the attached Word document [or: the following
document content]. Structure as a [INSERT NUMBER:
8-12] slide presentation with: 1) Executive Summary
slide (key findings and recommendations in 3 bullet
points), 2) Strategic Context slides (current
situation and market factors), 3) Core Analysis
slides (main findings with supporting data), 4)
Strategic Recommendations slides (specific actions
and rationale), 5) Implementation Overview slide
(timeline and resource requirements), 6) Next Steps
slide (immediate actions and decision points).
```

```
Focus on strategic implications rather than
operational details. Design each slide around one
key message that supports executive
decision-making. Include suggested slide titles and
2-3 bullet points of content for each slide.
```

Why This Prompt Works:

- **Persona Precision:** "Executive presentation specialist" ensures appropriate level of strategic focus rather than operational detail
- **Structured Framework:** Six-category approach covers all essential strategic presentation components
- **Decision Focus:** "Supports executive decision-making" filters content for leadership-appropriate insights
- **Slide Structure:** Specific format requirements ensure consistent, professional presentation organization

Category 2: Data Report Visualization

Data report visualization converts analytical documents and numerical summaries into presentation formats that make complex data accessible to diverse audiences.

Ready-to-Use Data Visualization Prompt:

```
None
Act as a data storytelling expert creating
presentation narratives from analytical reports.
Generate a [INSERT NUMBER: 6-10] slide presentation
outline from the attached data report [or:
following analytical content]. Structure with: 1)
Key Findings Overview (top 3-5 insights in summary
```

format), 2) Trend Analysis slides (patterns and changes over time), 3) Performance Highlights slides (achievements and notable results), 4) Challenge Areas slides (concerns requiring attention), 5) Comparative Analysis slides (benchmarks and context), 6) Strategic Implications slide (what this data means for business decisions). For each slide, provide the main headline, 2-3 supporting data points, and suggested chart or visual type. Focus on telling the story behind the numbers rather than displaying raw data.

Category 3: Process Documentation Presentation

Process documentation presentation adapts procedural documents and training materials into instructional slide sequences suitable for team education and stakeholder communication.

Ready-to-Use Process Documentation Prompt:

None
Act as a training and communication specialist converting procedural documentation into educational presentations. Create a [INSERT NUMBER: 8-15] slide presentation outline from the attached process document [or: following procedural content]. Organize as: 1) Process Overview slide (purpose and scope), 2) Prerequisites slides (requirements and preparation needed), 3) Step-by-Step Process slides (sequential phases with key actions), 4) Decision Points slides (where choices must be made), 5) Quality Controls slides (checkpoints and verification steps), 6)

Troubleshooting slide (common issues and solutions), 7) Resources and Support slide (contacts and additional information). Structure each process slide with clear action items and expected outcomes. Design for audience comprehension and retention rather than comprehensive technical detail.

Category 4: Proposal and Pitch Development

Proposal and pitch development creates persuasive presentations from project proposals and business case documents, optimizing content for stakeholder buy-in and decision approval.

Ready-to-Use Proposal Presentation Prompt:

None

Act as a business development specialist creating persuasive pitch presentations. Transform the attached proposal document [or: following proposal content] into a compelling [INSERT NUMBER: 8-12] slide presentation with: 1) Problem Statement slide (challenge and opportunity), 2) Proposed Solution slides (approach and methodology), 3) Benefits and Value slides (outcomes and ROI), 4) Implementation Plan slides (timeline and milestones), 5) Resource Requirements slide (investment and team needs), 6) Success Metrics slide (measurement and evaluation), 7) Call to Action slide (decision request and next steps). Focus on persuasive messaging that addresses stakeholder concerns and demonstrates clear value proposition. Include compelling headlines and supporting evidence for each key point.

Category 5: Update and Review Formatting

Update and review formatting structures status reports and progress summaries into stakeholder presentation formats that facilitate productive discussion and decision-making.

Ready-to-Use Status Update Prompt:

```
None
Act as a project communication specialist creating stakeholder update presentations. Convert the attached status report [or: following update content] into a [INSERT NUMBER: 6-10] slide presentation outline with: 1) Project Status Overview (current phase and overall progress), 2) Accomplishments slides (completed deliverables and achievements), 3) Current Activities slides (work in progress and focus areas), 4) Challenges and Issues slides (obstacles and proposed solutions), 5) Upcoming Milestones slides (next deliverables and timeline), 6) Decisions Needed slide (stakeholder input required). Structure each slide to facilitate productive discussion rather than passive information sharing. Include suggested discussion questions or decision points where stakeholder engagement is needed.
```

Implementation Workflow

Step 1: Prepare Source Document Access

1. Open Microsoft PowerPoint desktop application or web version
2. Ensure your source document is accessible (Word file, PDF, or text content)
3. Create a new blank presentation to work with
4. Access Copilot feature within PowerPoint interface

Step 2: Execute Document Analysis

1. Select appropriate prompt template based on your document type
2. Customize the slide count and specific requirements for your presentation needs
3. Insert or attach your source document as specified in the prompt
4. Submit the complete prompt to PowerPoint Copilot

Step 3: Process Generated Outline

1. Review the generated presentation structure and slide titles
2. Verify logical flow and completeness of key content areas
3. Note any additional slides or topics requiring manual addition
4. Use outline as foundation for slide development

Step 4: Refine and Customize

1. Adjust slide sequence based on your specific audience and objectives
2. Expand bullet points into full slide content using additional Copilot prompts
3. Identify slides requiring data visualizations or supporting graphics
4. Create final presentation structure ready for content development

Advanced Cross-Application Techniques

Sequential Document Processing: For complex presentations requiring multiple source documents, apply prompts sequentially:

1. **Primary Document:** Generate core presentation structure using main report or document
2. **Supporting Data:** Add analytical slides using Excel data or supplementary reports
3. **Strategic Context:** Enhance with market intelligence or external research documents
4. **Integration:** Combine multiple outlines into comprehensive presentation framework

Multi-Format Document Integration: Use this prompt for presentations requiring diverse source materials:

```
None
Act as a strategic communication consultant
creating comprehensive presentations from multiple
source documents. I will provide [INSERT NUMBER]
different documents covering various aspects of
[INSERT TOPIC/PROJECT]. Create a unified [INSERT
NUMBER] slide presentation outline that integrates
insights from all sources with: 1) Comprehensive
Overview (synthesizing all key themes), 2)
Integrated Analysis (combining insights across
documents), 3) Comparative Perspectives
(highlighting different viewpoints or data
sources), 4) Unified Recommendations (strategic
actions supported by all sources), 5)
Implementation Roadmap (combining timelines and
requirements from all materials). Ensure logical
flow and eliminate redundancy while maintaining
comprehensive coverage of all critical information.
```

Quick Win Testing Protocol

Test 1: Strategic Document Conversion (10 minutes)

1. Select a recent business report or strategic document from your files
2. Apply the Strategic Document Conversion prompt with 8-10 slide specification
3. Compare generated outline with manual presentation creation time and coverage
4. Use structured outline to develop actual presentation and measure efficiency gains

Test 2: Data Report Visualization (10 minutes)

1. Choose an Excel-based report or analytical document requiring presentation
2. Execute the Data Visualization prompt focusing on story-telling approach
3. Assess how systematic outline creation improves data presentation quality
4. Note enhanced narrative flow compared to traditional data dump presentations

Test 3: Cross-Application Workflow (15 minutes)

1. Apply the Multi-Format Document Integration prompt using 2-3 different source documents
2. Generate comprehensive presentation outline integrating diverse information sources
3. Measure time savings compared to manual synthesis and organization process
4. Evaluate improved presentation cohesion and strategic messaging quality

These systematic document-to-presentation prompts transform PowerPoint Copilot into your presentation development engine, converting complex documents into structured, audience-appropriate slide frameworks within minutes. You now possess the technical capability to generate compelling presentation outlines from any business document, eliminating blank-page paralysis while ensuring comprehensive coverage and logical flow that positions you as the collaborative professional who delivers strategic presentations consistently and efficiently.

3.2.2 Generating Speaker Notes and Key Talking Points

Presentation delivery represents the critical gap between compelling content and successful stakeholder engagement. Research indicates that 75% of professionals experience presentation anxiety, while 68% report feeling unprepared despite hours of slide development. The average presenter spends 3-4 hours creating slides but only 20-30 minutes preparing delivery materials, creating a fundamental imbalance that undermines presentation effectiveness.

Traditional speaker preparation involves manually crafting talking points from slide content, often resulting in reading directly from slides or relying on improvised commentary that lacks strategic messaging consistency. Most professionals struggle to translate visual slide elements into compelling verbal narratives that engage audiences while maintaining professional credibility.

PowerPoint Copilot transforms presentation delivery preparation from manual talking point creation into systematic speaker enhancement that generates audience-specific messaging, confident delivery guidance, and strategic narrative frameworks. You will master structured prompts that convert slide content into professional speaker notes, compelling talking points, and delivery confidence tools that position you as the prepared presenter who commands attention and drives results.

Core Speaker Enhancement Categories

Effective presentation delivery requires systematic support across five essential speaking dimensions:

- **Talking Point Generation:** Converting slide content into compelling verbal narratives
- **Audience-Specific Messaging:** Adapting delivery style for different stakeholder groups
- **Confidence Building Content:** Creating speaker notes that reduce anxiety and improve flow
- **Engagement Enhancement:** Developing interactive elements and audience connection strategies
- **Technical Content Translation:** Simplifying complex information for clear verbal communication

Category 1: Core Talking Point Generation

Core talking point generation transforms slide content into structured verbal narratives that enhance rather than duplicate visual elements, creating compelling delivery frameworks.

Ready-to-Use Talking Point Generation Prompt:

```
None
Act as a professional presentation coach developing
speaker talking points. For the slide titled
"[INSERT SLIDE TITLE]" with the following content:
[INSERT SLIDE CONTENT], generate 3-4 key talking
points that: 1) Expand on the slide content without
reading it verbatim, 2) Include specific examples
or context that support the main message, 3) Create
natural transitions to engage the audience, 4)
Maintain a professional and confident tone
throughout. Structure each talking point as a
complete thought that can stand alone, beginning
with a strong opening statement followed by
supporting detail. Focus on verbal delivery that
complements rather than repeats the visual content.
```

Why This Prompt Works:

- **Persona Precision:** "Professional presentation coach" ensures delivery-focused rather than content-focused approach
- **Complementary Strategy:** "Expand without reading verbatim" creates added value beyond slide text
- **Structure Specification:** "Complete thought that can stand alone" enables flexible presentation flow
- **Engagement Focus:** Natural transitions and audience connection enhance delivery effectiveness

Category 2: Audience-Specific Messaging Adaptation

Audience-specific messaging adaptation customizes talking points and delivery style for different stakeholder groups, ensuring appropriate tone and content depth for maximum impact.

Ready-to-Use Executive Audience Prompt:

```
None
Act as an executive communication specialist
preparing high-level presentation delivery. For the
slide on "[INSERT SLIDE TOPIC]", create speaker
notes tailored for an executive audience including
C-level leaders and senior stakeholders. Generate:
1) Strategic Context (why this information matters
at the strategic level), 2) Key Talking Points (3-4
high-impact messages focused on business
implications), 3) Supporting Evidence (data or
examples that executives find credible), 4)
Decision Relevance (how this information affects
choices they need to make). Use confident,
authoritative language that demonstrates
executive-level thinking. Focus on outcomes,
```

impact, and strategic implications rather than operational details.

Ready-to-Use Technical Team Prompt:

None

Act as a technical presentation specialist creating detailed delivery content. For the slide covering "[INSERT TECHNICAL TOPIC]", develop comprehensive speaker notes for a technical audience of specialists and practitioners. Include: 1) Technical Accuracy Points (precise details and specifications), 2) Implementation Insights (how this applies to their work), 3) Problem-Solving Context (challenges this addresses), 4) Interactive Elements (questions or discussion prompts to engage technical expertise). Use technically appropriate language that demonstrates subject matter expertise while maintaining clear explanation flow. Focus on practical application and technical depth.

Category 3: Confidence Building Speaker Notes

Confidence building speaker notes provide comprehensive delivery guidance that reduces presentation anxiety while ensuring smooth, professional presentation flow.

Ready-to-Use Comprehensive Speaker Notes Prompt:

None

Act as a presentation confidence coach creating detailed speaker notes. For this presentation slide on "[INSERT SLIDE TOPIC]", generate comprehensive speaker guidance including: 1) Opening Statement (strong, attention-grabbing first sentence), 2) Main Content Flow (logical sequence of 3-4 talking points with smooth transitions), 3) Audience Engagement Moments (specific points to make eye contact, pause, or invite interaction), 4) Backup Information (additional details if questions arise), 5) Transition to Next Slide (natural bridge to continue presentation flow). Write in a confident, professional tone that gives the speaker clear guidance for every moment. Include timing estimates and delivery cues where helpful.

Category 4: Engagement Enhancement Techniques

Engagement enhancement techniques create interactive elements and audience connection strategies that transform passive presentations into dynamic collaborative experiences.

Ready-to-Use Audience Engagement Prompt:

None

Act as an audience engagement specialist developing interactive presentation elements. For the slide about "[INSERT SLIDE CONTENT]", create speaker notes that include: 1) Opening Engagement Hook (question, statistic, or scenario that captures attention), 2) Interactive Moments (specific points to ask questions or request audience input), 3) Storytelling Elements (brief anecdotes or examples that make content relatable), 4) Call-to-Action Opportunities (ways audience can apply or respond to the information), 5) Energy Maintenance Tips (techniques to keep audience attention throughout). Focus on creating genuine connection and participation rather than forced interaction. Ensure all engagement elements serve the core message and objectives.

Category 5: Technical Content Translation

Technical content translation simplifies complex information into accessible verbal communication that maintains accuracy while enhancing audience comprehension.

Ready-to-Use Technical Translation Prompt:

None
Act as a technical communication expert specializing in complex content translation. For the technical slide covering "[INSERT TECHNICAL TOPIC]", create speaker notes that translate complex concepts for a mixed audience including both technical and non-technical stakeholders. Structure with: 1) Simple Overview (non-technical explanation of the main concept), 2) Technical Detail Layer (more specific information for technical audience members), 3) Analogy or Metaphor (relatable comparison to help understanding), 4) Practical Impact Explanation (why this matters in business terms), 5) Question Preparation (anticipated questions and clear answers). Maintain

technical accuracy while ensuring accessibility for all audience skill levels.

Implementation Workflow

Step 1: Access PowerPoint Copilot for Speaker Support

1. Open your completed PowerPoint presentation
2. Navigate to the slide requiring speaker enhancement
3. Access Copilot feature within PowerPoint interface
4. Ensure slide content is finalized before generating speaker notes

Step 2: Execute Slide-by-Slide Enhancement

1. Apply Core Talking Point Generation prompt to each major slide
2. Customize audience-specific messaging based on your presentation context
3. Generate comprehensive speaker notes for complex or critical slides
4. Create engagement elements for key interaction opportunities

Step 3: Build Complete Speaker Package

1. Combine individual slide talking points into cohesive presentation narrative
2. Add transition language between major sections
3. Include timing guidance and delivery cues throughout
4. Create backup content for potential questions or extended discussion

Step 4: Practice and Refinement Process

1. Review generated speaker notes for flow and consistency
2. Practice delivery using structured talking points
3. Adjust timing and emphasis based on rehearsal feedback
4. Finalize speaker notes for confident presentation delivery

Advanced Speaker Enhancement Techniques

Sequential Enhancement Process: For high-stakes presentations, apply prompts systematically across presentation structure:

1. **Opening Strong:** Generate compelling introduction talking points
2. **Content Flow:** Develop smooth transitions and engaging main content
3. **Audience Connection:** Add engagement elements throughout presentation
4. **Closing Impact:** Create memorable conclusion and call-to-action messaging

Multi-Audience Preparation: Use this prompt for presentations requiring different delivery approaches:

```
None
Act as a presentation versatility specialist
preparing speaker notes for multiple audience
scenarios. For the slide on "[INSERT SLIDE TOPIC]",
create three versions of talking points: 1)
Executive Version (strategic focus, business
impact, decision relevance), 2) Technical Version
(detailed specifications, implementation focus,
problem-solving context), 3) General Business
Version (balanced approach, practical applications,
accessible language). For each version, provide 2-3
key talking points that maintain the same core
message while adapting depth and focus for audience
expertise level. Include guidance on which version
to use based on audience composition.
```

Quick Win Testing Protocol

Test 1: Talking Point Generation (5 minutes)

1. Select a content-heavy slide from an existing presentation
2. Apply the Core Talking Point Generation prompt with specific slide content
3. Compare generated talking points with your typical preparation approach
4. Practice delivery using structured talking points and assess confidence improvement

Test 2: Audience-Specific Adaptation (5 minutes)

1. Choose a technical or complex slide requiring audience adaptation
2. Execute both Executive Audience and Technical Team prompts for the same content
3. Note how systematic adaptation improves message relevance and delivery effectiveness
4. Use adapted talking points for actual stakeholder presentation

Test 3: Complete Speaker Enhancement (10 minutes)

1. Apply the full speaker enhancement workflow to a 5-slide presentation sequence
2. Generate comprehensive speaker notes, engagement elements, and transition guidance
3. Measure preparation time reduction compared to manual speaker note creation
4. Deliver enhanced presentation and observe improved confidence and audience engagement

These systematic speaker enhancement prompts transform PowerPoint Copilot into your presentation delivery coach, converting slide content into confident, engaging, and audience-appropriate verbal communication. You now possess the technical capability to generate professional speaker notes, compelling talking points, and delivery confidence tools that position you as the prepared presenter who commands attention, engages audiences effectively, and drives successful presentation outcomes consistently.

4. Amplify Your Analytical Power

You have mastered the collaborative dimensions of professional productivity through systematic meeting preparation, strategic presentation development, and systematic follow-up execution. Your PTCF Framework now operates seamlessly across Teams and PowerPoint, transforming you from reactive participant to proactive collaboration leader who commands meeting effectiveness and drives stakeholder engagement.

The next frontier in your AI-powered productivity transformation addresses the analytical challenges that separate tactical contributors from strategic decision-makers. Data analysis and strategic insight generation represent the most intimidating yet potentially transformative applications of Microsoft 365 Copilot. This chapter positions you to become the data-driven strategist who uncovers hidden patterns, generates compelling insights, and makes informed decisions that drive organizational success.

The Data Analysis Intimidation Barrier

Data analysis paralyzes most professionals despite its critical importance for strategic advancement. Research indicates that 73% of knowledge workers avoid complex data interpretation tasks, while 68% report feeling overwhelmed when asked to extract insights from spreadsheets containing more than basic calculations. The average professional spends less than 15 minutes weekly on analytical thinking, relegating strategic insight generation to specialized data analysts or postponing critical decisions indefinitely.

Traditional Excel analysis requires technical expertise that most professionals lack: advanced formula construction, pivot table manipulation, statistical function knowledge, and data visualization skills. These barriers create systematic analytical avoidance that limits career advancement and undermines decision-making quality. Professionals resort to surface-level observations, gut instinct choices, and delayed strategic responses that erode competitive advantage.

The analytical skills gap extends beyond individual limitations to organizational effectiveness. Companies report that 84% of strategic decisions rely on incomplete data analysis, while 59% of critical business choices occur without adequate quantitative foundation. This analytical deficit costs organizations millions in missed opportunities, misallocated resources, and strategic missteps that could be prevented through systematic data interrogation.

I have observed this analytical paralysis across international consulting engagements. A senior director at a multinational technology firm once confided that she avoided quarterly business reviews because she felt unable to generate meaningful insights from performance data. Her team's Excel reports contained comprehensive metrics, but translating numbers into strategic recommendations exceeded her technical capabilities. This analytical confidence gap limited her executive presence and strategic contribution despite strong leadership skills in other areas.

The Strategic Insight Opportunity

Excel Copilot transforms data analysis from technical barrier into strategic advantage through natural language interaction that eliminates formula complexity while maintaining analytical sophistication. You will master systematic approaches that convert overwhelming datasets into clear insights, complex calculations into simple requests, and scattered information into compelling strategic narratives.

The AI augmentation opportunity in analytical work exceeds any other Microsoft 365 application because data analysis amplifies decision-making quality across every professional dimension. Strategic insights inform budget allocation, resource deployment, market positioning, and operational optimization. Professionals who master AI-powered analysis gain competitive advantage through superior decision support and strategic recommendation capability.

Microsoft 365 Copilot in Excel operates as your personal data scientist, capable of performing complex statistical analysis, identifying trend patterns, generating predictive insights, and creating compelling visualizations without requiring advanced technical knowledge. The PTCF Framework applies perfectly to analytical tasks: Persona defines the analytical role perspective, Task specifies the insight objectives, Context provides business parameters, and Format ensures actionable output delivery.

Your analytical transformation using Copilot creates exponential rather than incremental productivity gains. Unlike communication and meeting efficiency improvements that save time, analytical mastery generates new strategic value that enhances decision quality and competitive positioning. You transition from data consumer to insight generator, from reactive reporter to proactive strategist.

System 1: The Data Interrogation Engine

The Data Interrogation Engine leverages Excel Copilot to extract precise answers from complex datasets through systematic questioning approaches that eliminate manual calculation requirements while ensuring analytical accuracy. This system transforms spreadsheet intimidation into confident data exploration.

Traditional Excel analysis requires predetermined questions and technical formula knowledge that limit analytical exploration. The Data Interrogation Engine reverses this process: you formulate business questions in natural language, and Copilot generates the analytical framework needed to provide comprehensive answers. This approach encourages deeper data exploration and reveals insights that manual analysis often misses.

You will master prompts that generate complex formulas from simple descriptions, identify statistical patterns without advanced mathematics knowledge, and create comparative analyses that illuminate business performance trends. The system encompasses everything from basic calculation generation to sophisticated trend analysis that supports strategic decision-making.

The Data Interrogation Engine operates through systematic prompt categories that address different analytical needs: Formula Generation for complex calculations, Pattern Recognition for trend identification, Comparative Analysis for performance benchmarking, and Outlier Detection for anomaly investigation. Each category employs PTCF Framework principles to ensure precise, actionable analytical output.

System 2: The Strategic Insights Generator

The Strategic Insights Generator extends beyond data analysis into strategic synthesis that converts analytical findings into business recommendations and high-level strategic guidance. This system positions you as the professional who transforms numbers into strategy.

Strategic insight generation requires business context understanding that pure data analysis cannot provide. The Strategic Insights Generator combines Copilot's analytical capabilities with business strategy frameworks to generate SWOT analyses, competitive assessments, market opportunity evaluations, and strategic recommendations that inform executive decision-making.

You will develop expertise in cross-application workflows that synthesize information from multiple sources into comprehensive strategic briefings. These capabilities include processing market research into actionable insights, converting operational data into strategic recommendations, and generating executive-level summaries that support critical business decisions.

The Strategic Insights Generator employs advanced PTCF Framework applications that specify strategic analyst personas, complex analytical tasks, comprehensive business contexts, and executive-appropriate output formats. This system produces insights that rival professional consulting analysis while requiring no specialized training or technical expertise.

The Analytical Transformation Promise

This chapter delivers your transition from data-intimidated professional to confident analytical strategist through systematic mastery of two comprehensive systems. You will learn to interrogate any dataset with precision, generate insights that inform strategic decisions, and create analytical narratives that enhance your professional credibility and strategic value.

The Data Interrogation Engine provides immediate tactical advantages: faster calculation completion, accurate trend identification, and confident data manipulation that eliminates analytical avoidance behaviors. You will approach spreadsheets with curiosity rather than apprehension, knowing that Copilot provides the technical capability needed to extract meaningful insights.

The Strategic Insights Generator creates long-term strategic advantages: enhanced decision-making quality, improved strategic recommendation capability, and increased executive presence through analytical competence. You will generate insights that inform organizational strategy, support resource allocation decisions, and drive competitive advantage through superior business intelligence.

Your analytical mastery using the PTCF Framework positions you as the professional who bridges operational data and strategic insight, connecting quantitative analysis with qualitative business understanding. This capability distinguishes you from peers who remain trapped in either pure data manipulation or unsupported strategic speculation.

The transformation extends beyond individual productivity to organizational impact. Your enhanced analytical capabilities enable better team decision-making, more accurate forecasting, and strategic recommendations that drive business success. You become the collaborative leader who brings data-driven insights to strategic discussions and executive presentations.

Upon completing this chapter, you will possess systematic approaches for converting any business question into precise analytical investigation, transforming raw data into strategic recommendations, and generating executive-level insights that enhance your professional impact and organizational value. The analytical confidence you develop here amplifies every other professional capability while positioning you for strategic leadership advancement.

4.1 THE DATA INTERROGATION ENGINE

4.1.1 GENERATING FORMULAS FROM NATURAL LANGUAGE DESCRIPTIONS

Excel formula construction represents the greatest technical barrier preventing professionals from leveraging spreadsheet analytical power. Research indicates that 89% of Excel users employ fewer than 10% of available formula functions, while 76% report avoiding complex calculations due to syntax intimidation. The average professional spends 45 minutes researching and testing a single advanced formula, often abandoning analytical tasks entirely when formulas fail to execute correctly.

Traditional Excel mastery requires memorizing hundreds of function names, understanding nested parentheses logic, mastering cell reference syntax, and debugging cryptic error messages that provide minimal guidance for resolution. These technical barriers transform data analysis from strategic advantage into frustrating obstacle course that consumes time while delivering inconsistent results.

Excel Copilot eliminates formula construction complexity through natural language interpretation that converts business questions into precise mathematical expressions. You will master systematic prompts that generate complex formulas without requiring syntax knowledge, function memorization, or debugging expertise while maintaining complete analytical accuracy.

Core Formula Generation Categories

Effective natural language formula generation requires systematic approaches across six essential calculation types:

- **Basic Mathematical Operations:** Addition, subtraction, multiplication, division, and percentage calculations

- **Logical Operations:** IF statements, conditional logic, and comparison functions
- **Lookup Functions:** VLOOKUP, HLOOKUP, INDEX MATCH, and cross-reference calculations
- **Statistical Analysis:** Averages, counts, summations, and distribution calculations
- **Date and Time Functions:** Duration calculations, scheduling logic, and temporal analysis
- **Advanced Analytics:** Compound formulas, nested functions, and multi-criteria analysis

Category 1: Basic Mathematical Operations

Basic mathematical operations form the foundation of Excel analytical capability, encompassing percentage calculations, variance analysis, and comparative metrics that inform business decisions.

Ready-to-Use Percentage Change Calculation Prompt:

```
None
Act as an Excel formula specialist creating
percentage change calculations. I need a formula in
column G that calculates the percentage change
between the values in column E (previous period)
and column F (current period). Structure the
formula to: 1) Handle zero values in the previous
period appropriately, 2) Display results as
percentages with two decimal places, 3) Show
positive changes as positive numbers and negative
changes as negative numbers. Provide the exact
formula syntax and explain each component of the
calculation logic.
```

Ready-to-Use Growth Rate Analysis Prompt:

```
None
Act  as  a  financial  analyst  creating  growth
calculations. Generate a formula for column H that
calculates the compound annual growth rate (CAGR)
between the starting value in column C and ending
value in column D, with the number of periods
specified in column E. The formula should: 1) Use
the standard CAGR mathematical formula, 2) Handle
cases where starting values might be negative, 3)
Display  results  as  percentages.  Include  the
complete formula and explanation of how it works.
```

Category 2: Logical Operations and Conditional Analysis

Logical operations enable sophisticated decision-making within spreadsheets through conditional logic that automates business rule implementation and exception handling.

Ready-to-Use Multi-Criteria IF Statement Prompt:

```
None
Act  as  a  business  logic  specialist  creating
conditional formulas. I need a formula in column I
that  evaluates  multiple  conditions  and  returns
different  text  values  based  on  performance
criteria. The logic should be: IF column F (sales
amount) is greater than 10000 AND column G (region)
equals "North", return "Top Performer", IF column F
is between 5000 and 10000, return "Good", otherwise
return "Needs Improvement". Provide the complete
nested IF formula with proper syntax and logical
operators.
```

Ready-to-Use Status Classification Prompt:

None

Act as a project management specialist creating status tracking formulas. Create a formula for column J that assigns project status based on multiple criteria: IF column E (completion percentage) is 100%, return "Complete", IF column F (due date) is past today's date and completion is less than 100%, return "Overdue", IF completion is greater than 75%, return "On Track", otherwise return "At Risk". Include the formula with proper date functions and logical nesting.

Category 3: Lookup Functions and Data Integration

Lookup functions enable cross-referencing data between sheets and tables, creating dynamic connections that maintain accuracy while reducing manual data entry requirements.

Ready-to-Use VLOOKUP Data Integration Prompt:

None

Act as a database integration specialist creating lookup formulas. I need a VLOOKUP formula in column H that pulls data from the "Sales" worksheet. The formula should: 1) Look up the value in column A of the current row, 2) Search for this value in the first column of the range A:D on the Sales sheet, 3) Return the value from the 3rd column of that range, 4) Use exact match only. Include error handling with IFERROR to display "Not Found" when the lookup fails. Provide the complete formula with proper sheet references.

Ready-to-Use Advanced INDEX MATCH Prompt:

None

Act as an Excel expert creating flexible lookup formulas. Create an INDEX MATCH formula for column I that offers more flexibility than VLOOKUP. The formula should: 1) Look up the value in column B, 2) Search the range "Products!A:A" for matches, 3) Return corresponding values from "Products!C:C", 4) Handle exact matches only, 5) Include error handling for missing values. Explain why INDEX MATCH is more powerful than VLOOKUP and provide the complete syntax.

Category 4: Statistical Analysis and Aggregation

Statistical analysis functions provide business intelligence through data summarization, trend identification, and performance measurement calculations.

Ready-to-Use Multi-Criteria SUMIFS Prompt:

None

Act as a data analyst creating complex aggregation formulas. I need a SUMIFS formula in cell G2 that calculates total sales based on multiple criteria: 1) Sum values from column E (sales amounts), 2) Where column B (product category) equals the value in cell F1, 3) AND where column C (region) equals the value in cell F2, 4) AND where column D (date) is within the current year. Provide the complete SUMIFS formula with proper range references and criteria syntax.

Ready-to-Use Statistical Summary Prompt:

```
None
Act as a statistical analyst creating comprehensive
data summaries. Create formulas for cells H1
through H5 that calculate: H1 = COUNT of non-empty
values in column E, H2 = AVERAGE of values in
column E, H3 = MAX value in column E, H4 = MIN
value in column E, H5 = STDEV (standard deviation)
of values in column E. Include proper error
handling for empty datasets and provide all five
formulas with clear labels.
```

Category 5: Date and Time Analysis

Date and time functions enable temporal analysis, scheduling calculations, and duration measurements that support project management and operational planning.

Ready-to-Use Business Days Calculation Prompt:

```
None
Act as a project scheduling specialist creating
date calculations. I need formulas for columns F
and G: Column F should calculate the number of
business days between the start date in column D
and end date in column E, excluding weekends.
Column G should calculate the target completion
date by adding the number of business days in
column C to the start date in column B. Use
NETWORKDAYS for the first formula and WORKDAY for
the second. Include proper error handling for
invalid dates.
```

Ready-to-Use Age and Duration Prompt:

```
None
Act as a data analysis expert creating time-based
calculations. Create formulas for columns H, I, and
J: Column H = calculate age in years from birth
date in column D to today, Column I = calculate
months between start date in column E and end date
in column F, Column J = calculate the day of the
week for the date in column G. Use DATEDIF, DATEDIF
with "M" parameter, and WEEKDAY functions
respectively. Provide complete formulas with proper
syntax.
```

Implementation Workflow

Step 1: Access Excel Copilot Formula Generation

1. Open Microsoft Excel desktop application or web version
2. Navigate to the cell where you need the formula
3. Click on the Copilot icon or use the formula bar integration
4. Ensure your data range is properly organized with clear column headers

Step 2: Execute Natural Language Formula Request

1. Select the appropriate prompt template based on your calculation needs
2. Customize the prompt with your specific column references and criteria
3. Submit the complete prompt to Excel Copilot
4. Review the generated formula for accuracy and completeness

Step 3: Test and Validate Formula Results

1. Apply the generated formula to a test cell with known data
2. Verify the calculation results match your expected outcomes
3. Test edge cases like empty cells, zero values, and error conditions
4. Copy the validated formula to additional cells as needed

Step 4: Document and Reuse Successful Formulas

1. Save working formulas in your personal prompt library
2. Document the business logic and use cases for each formula type
3. Create template versions for recurring analytical needs
4. Share successful formulas with team members for consistent analysis

Advanced Formula Generation Techniques

Complex Nested Function Creation: For sophisticated calculations requiring multiple function layers, use this systematic approach:

```
None
Act as an advanced Excel specialist creating complex nested formulas. I need a formula that combines multiple functions to achieve the following business logic: [INSERT DETAILED REQUIREMENTS]. Break down the solution into: 1) The outer function that controls the main logic, 2) The inner functions that handle specific calculations, 3) Error handling for edge cases, 4) Formatting requirements for the output. Provide the complete nested formula with clear explanation of each component and how they work together.
```

Quick Win Testing Protocol

Test 1: Percentage Change Formula (5 minutes)

1. Create two columns with sample numerical data representing before and after values
2. Apply the Percentage Change Calculation prompt to generate the formula
3. Verify the calculation accuracy by manually checking a few results
4. Test edge cases including zero values and negative numbers

Test 2: VLOOKUP Data Integration (5 minutes)

1. Set up a simple lookup table on a separate worksheet
2. Use the VLOOKUP Data Integration prompt to create a cross-reference formula
3. Test the lookup functionality with both existing and non-existing values
4. Verify error handling displays appropriate messages for missing data

Test 3: Multi-Criteria Analysis (10 minutes)

1. Apply the Multi-Criteria SUMIFS prompt to a dataset with multiple filtering needs
2. Verify the formula correctly aggregates data based on your specified criteria
3. Test different criteria combinations to ensure formula flexibility
4. Compare results with manual filtering to confirm accuracy

These systematic natural language formula generation prompts transform Excel Copilot into your personal formula expert, eliminating syntax barriers while maintaining complete analytical precision. You now possess the technical capability to generate complex calculations through simple business language descriptions, positioning you as the data-confident professional who approaches analytical challenges with systematic formula mastery rather than technical intimidation.

4.1.2 Identifying Key Trends and Outliers in Datasets

Data pattern recognition represents the analytical skill gap that separates tactical contributors from strategic decision-makers. Research indicates that 82% of professionals avoid pattern analysis in complex datasets, while 71% report feeling overwhelmed when asked to identify trends beyond basic sorting and filtering. The average business professional spends less than 10 minutes monthly on meaningful data exploration, missing critical insights that could inform strategic decisions and competitive advantages.

Traditional Excel trend analysis requires advanced statistical knowledge, pivot table expertise, chart construction skills, and pattern recognition experience that most professionals lack. These barriers create systematic analytical avoidance that limits career advancement while allowing competitors to exploit overlooked opportunities hidden within accessible business data.

Excel Copilot transforms trend identification from technical obstacles into strategic conversation through natural language analysis that reveals patterns, highlights anomalies, and generates insights without requiring statistical expertise or advanced Excel knowledge. You will master systematic prompts that position Copilot as your personal data analyst, capable of uncovering trends and outliers that inform decision-making and drive business results.

Core Data Analysis Categories

Effective trend and outlier identification requires systematic approaches across five essential analytical dimensions:

- **Performance Ranking Analysis:** Identifying top and bottom performers across metrics and categories
- **Trend Pattern Recognition:** Detecting growth, decline, seasonal, and cyclical patterns in time-series data

- **Outlier and Anomaly Detection:** Locating unusual values that warrant investigation or represent opportunities
- **Comparative Analysis:** Benchmarking performance across categories, periods, and segments
- **Distribution and Correlation Analysis:** Understanding data spread, clustering, and relationship patterns

Category 1: Performance Ranking and Top Performer Analysis

Performance ranking analysis identifies highest and lowest performing elements across business metrics, enabling resource allocation decisions and strategic focus areas.

Ready-to-Use Top Performer Analysis Prompt:

```
None
Act as a business performance analyst examining
this dataset for key insights. Analyze this table
and highlight the top 5 performing products by
revenue, along with the bottom 5 performers. For
each group, provide: 1) The specific values and
rankings, 2) The percentage of total revenue each
represents, 3) Notable characteristics or patterns
you observe, 4) Potential business implications of
these performance levels. Structure your analysis
in a clear summary format that highlights the most
significant findings for business decision-making.
```

Ready-to-Use Multi-Metric Performance Prompt:

```
None
Act as a comprehensive business analyst conducting
performance evaluation. Examine this data and
identify the top performers across multiple
```

metrics: highest revenue, highest units sold, and highest profit margin. Create a summary showing: 1) Which items appear in multiple top performer categories, 2) Any items that rank high in one metric but low in another, 3) The overall performance leaders when considering all metrics together, 4) Recommendations for which products deserve increased focus and resources. Highlight any surprising findings that warrant strategic attention.

Category 2: Trend Pattern Recognition and Time-Series Analysis

Trend pattern recognition reveals temporal changes, seasonal variations, and directional movements that inform forecasting and strategic planning decisions.

Ready-to-Use Trend Analysis Prompt:

None

Act as a trend analysis specialist examining temporal patterns in business data. Analyze this dataset for time-based trends and patterns. Identify: 1) Overall directional trends (growth, decline, or stability), 2) Seasonal patterns or cyclical variations, 3) Notable acceleration or deceleration points, 4) Periods of unusual performance that deviate from established patterns. Provide specific examples with dates and values, and explain what these trends might indicate for future business planning and strategic decisions.

Ready-to-Use Growth Rate Analysis Prompt:

```
None
Act as a growth analysis expert evaluating business
trajectory. Examine this time-series data and
calculate growth rates between periods. Highlight:
1) The periods with highest and lowest growth
rates, 2) Any periods showing negative growth or
concerning declines, 3) Consistent growth patterns
versus volatile performance, 4) Recent trends
compared to historical averages. Provide specific
percentage changes and identify which time periods
require management attention or represent
significant opportunities.
```

Category 3: Outlier and Anomaly Detection

Outlier detection identifies unusual values that may represent data errors, exceptional performance, or investigation opportunities requiring management attention.

Ready-to-Use Outlier Detection Prompt:

```
None
Act as a data quality and anomaly detection
specialist. Identify any unusual outliers in the
'Marketing Spend' column that I should investigate.
For each outlier identified: 1) Specify the exact
value and how it compares to typical ranges, 2)
Calculate how many standard deviations it
represents from the average, 3) Suggest potential
reasons for this unusual value (data error,
exceptional circumstance, or legitimate variation),
```

4) Recommend whether this requires immediate investigation or represents a normal business exception. Focus on actionable insights rather than just statistical measurements.

Ready-to-Use Multi-Column Anomaly Analysis Prompt:

None

Act as a comprehensive anomaly detection analyst examining multiple data columns for unusual patterns. Scan this dataset and identify any rows or entries that contain unusual combinations of values across different metrics. Look for: 1) Individual cells with extreme values relative to their column averages, 2) Rows where multiple metrics show unusual patterns simultaneously, 3) Logical inconsistencies between related columns, 4) Values that fall outside expected business ranges or relationships. Provide specific examples and assess whether these anomalies likely represent data errors or legitimate business exceptions requiring attention.

Category 4: Comparative Analysis and Benchmarking

Comparative analysis reveals performance differences across categories, segments, and time periods that inform resource allocation and strategic prioritization.

Ready-to-Use Category Comparison Prompt:

None

Act as a comparative business analyst evaluating performance across different categories. Compare the performance of different product categories, regions, or segments in this dataset. Provide: 1) Clear rankings showing which categories perform best across key metrics, 2) The percentage differences between top and bottom performing categories, 3) Categories showing consistent strength versus those with mixed performance, 4) Strategic recommendations for resource allocation based on these comparative insights. Include specific numbers and percentages to support your analysis.

Ready-to-Use Period-over-Period Comparison Prompt:

None

Act as a temporal analysis specialist comparing performance across different time periods. Examine this data and compare current period performance against previous periods. Highlight: 1) Metrics showing the most significant improvement or decline, 2) Categories or products with the most notable period-over-period changes, 3) Consistency of performance trends across different time comparisons, 4) Areas where recent performance differs substantially from historical patterns. Provide percentage changes and identify trends that require strategic response or represent emerging opportunities.

Category 5: Distribution and Relationship Analysis

Distribution analysis reveals data clustering, spread patterns, and correlational relationships that inform strategic understanding and decision-making.

Ready-to-Use Distribution Analysis Prompt:

```
None
Act as a statistical analyst examining data
distribution patterns. Analyze the distribution of
values in this dataset and describe: 1) The range
and spread of values across key metrics, 2) Whether
data clusters around certain values or spreads
evenly, 3) Any gaps or concentrations in the data
that represent business patterns, 4) The
relationship between different metrics and whether
high performance in one area correlates with
performance in others. Explain these patterns in
business terms rather than purely statistical
language.
```

Implementation Workflow

Step 1: Data Preparation and Access

1. Open your Excel dataset ensuring all relevant columns contain clean, organized data
2. Remove any empty rows or columns that might interfere with analysis
3. Verify column headers are clear and descriptive for Copilot interpretation
4. Access Excel Copilot through the ribbon interface or chat feature

Step 2: Execute Systematic Analysis Sequence

1. **Performance Overview:** Start with Top Performer Analysis to understand key contributors
2. **Trend Examination:** Apply Trend Analysis prompts to identify temporal patterns
3. **Anomaly Investigation:** Use Outlier Detection prompts to locate unusual values
4. **Comparative Insights:** Execute Comparison prompts to understand relative performance

Step 3: Generate Comprehensive Analysis Report

1. Combine insights from multiple prompt categories into cohesive narrative
2. Prioritize findings based on business impact and actionability
3. Create summary document highlighting key trends and recommended actions
4. Prepare presentation-ready insights for stakeholder communication

Step 4: Validate and Act on Insights

1. Cross-reference unusual findings with business context and domain knowledge
2. Investigate significant outliers to determine if they represent opportunities or errors
3. Develop action plans based on trend analysis and performance comparisons
4. Establish monitoring systems for ongoing trend tracking and analysis

Advanced Pattern Recognition Techniques

Multi-Dimensional Analysis: For comprehensive dataset examination across multiple variables simultaneously:

None

Act as an advanced business intelligence analyst conducting multi-dimensional analysis. Examine this dataset across all available metrics and identify complex patterns that involve relationships between multiple columns. Look for: 1) Combinations of factors that lead to exceptional performance, 2) Warning signs where multiple metrics show concerning patterns simultaneously, 3) Opportunities where strong performance in one area isn't being leveraged in related areas, 4) Strategic insights that only become apparent when examining multiple data dimensions together. Provide actionable recommendations based on these complex pattern insights.

Quick Win Testing Protocol

Test 1: Performance Ranking Analysis (5 minutes)

1. Select a dataset with clear performance metrics like sales, revenue, or productivity measures
2. Apply the Top Performer Analysis prompt to identify highest and lowest performers
3. Verify the rankings align with your business understanding and expectations
4. Use insights to inform resource allocation or recognition decisions

Test 2: Outlier Detection Validation (5 minutes)

1. Choose a dataset likely to contain unusual values or anomalies
2. Execute the Outlier Detection prompt targeting a specific column with potential irregularities

3. Investigate identified outliers to determine if they represent genuine issues or opportunities
4. Document findings for follow-up investigation or corrective action

Test 3: Trend Pattern Recognition (10 minutes)

1. Apply the Trend Analysis prompt to time-series data showing performance over multiple periods
2. Identify directional trends and seasonal patterns that inform future planning
3. Compare AI-identified trends with your intuitive understanding of business performance
4. Use trend insights to adjust strategic plans or operational focus areas

These systematic trend and outlier identification prompts transform Excel Copilot into your expert data analyst, revealing patterns and anomalies that inform strategic decisions without requiring advanced statistical knowledge. You now possess the analytical capability to interrogate any dataset for meaningful insights, positioning you as the data-confident professional who uncovers strategic opportunities hidden within business information while driving decision-making through systematic pattern recognition.

4.2 THE STRATEGIC INSIGHTS GENERATOR

4.2.1 CREATING SWOT ANALYSES FROM BUSINESS DOCUMENTS

Strategic analysis intimidates most professionals despite its critical importance for competitive positioning and decision-making. Research indicates that 79% of business professionals avoid conducting formal strategic assessments, while 67% report feeling overwhelmed when asked to analyze market opportunities and competitive threats. The average manager spends less than 30 minutes quarterly on strategic analysis activities, missing critical insights that could inform resource allocation and competitive advantage.

Traditional SWOT analysis requires strategic thinking expertise, market knowledge synthesis, competitive intelligence gathering, and business framework application that most professionals lack. These barriers create systematic strategic avoidance that limits career advancement while allowing competitors to exploit overlooked market positions and organizational capabilities.

Microsoft 365 Copilot transforms strategic analysis from intimidating exercise into systematic conversation through cross-application workflows that generate comprehensive SWOT assessments, competitive analyses, and strategic recommendations without requiring MBA-level strategic thinking expertise.

Core Strategic Analysis Categories

Effective SWOT generation requires systematic approaches across four essential strategic dimensions:

- **Comprehensive SWOT Framework Analysis:** Complete strengths, weaknesses, opportunities, and threats assessment

- **Competitive Positioning Analysis:** Market position evaluation and competitive advantage identification
- **Strategic Scenario Planning:** Future opportunity and risk assessment based on current capabilities
- **Cross-Document Strategic Synthesis:** Multi-source strategic intelligence integration and analysis

Category 1: Comprehensive SWOT Framework Analysis

Comprehensive SWOT analysis converts business documents into structured strategic assessments that identify internal capabilities and external market factors affecting organizational success.

Ready-to-Use Master SWOT Analysis Prompt:

```
None
Act as a senior business strategist and management
consultant conducting comprehensive strategic
analysis. Based on the attached business document
[or: the following business information], generate
a detailed SWOT analysis with the following
structure: 1) STRENGTHS: Internal capabilities,
resources, and advantages that provide competitive
benefits, 2) WEAKNESSES: Internal limitations,
resource gaps, and areas requiring improvement, 3)
OPPORTUNITIES: External market trends, customer
needs, and environmental factors that could be
leveraged for growth, 4) THREATS: External
challenges, competitive pressures, and market risks
that could impact performance. For each category,
provide 3-5 specific, actionable insights with
brief explanations of their strategic implications.
Conclude with 2-3 strategic priorities based on the
analysis.
```

Ready-to-Use Document-Specific SWOT Prompt:

```
None
Act as a strategic planning specialist analyzing
business documentation for strategic insights.
Review the attached [INSERT DOCUMENT TYPE: business
plan/market research report/financial
analysis/operational review] and create a focused
SWOT analysis that addresses: 1) STRENGTHS: What
unique capabilities, resources, or market positions
does this document reveal, 2) WEAKNESSES: What
gaps, limitations, or vulnerabilities are evident
in the analysis, 3) OPPORTUNITIES: What market
trends, customer insights, or growth possibilities
are identified, 4) THREATS: What competitive risks,
market challenges, or external pressures are
highlighted. Present findings in a clear
four-quadrant format with specific examples and
quantitative details where available.
```

Category 2: Competitive Positioning Analysis

Competitive positioning analysis leverages business intelligence documents to assess market position relative to competitors and identify strategic differentiation opportunities.

Ready-to-Use Competitive SWOT Prompt:

```
None
Act as a competitive intelligence analyst creating
strategic positioning assessments. Using the
provided business information, develop a
competition-focused SWOT analysis that emphasizes:
1) STRENGTHS: Competitive advantages and
differentiation factors versus market competitors,
2) WEAKNESSES: Areas where competitors outperform
```

or hold superior market positions, 3) OPPORTUNITIES: Market gaps, competitor vulnerabilities, or emerging segments where competitive advantage can be established, 4) THREATS: Competitive actions, new market entrants, or industry changes that could erode current market position. Include specific competitive comparisons and strategic recommendations for maintaining or improving competitive standing.

Category 3: Strategic Scenario Planning Analysis

Strategic scenario planning converts current business intelligence into future-focused strategic assessment that anticipates opportunities and challenges across multiple business environments.

Ready-to-Use Scenario-Based SWOT Prompt:

None

Act as a strategic planning expert conducting scenario-based analysis for future business planning. Based on the attached business documentation, create a forward-looking SWOT analysis that considers: 1) STRENGTHS: Current capabilities that will provide advantages in evolving market conditions, 2) WEAKNESSES: Current limitations that could become critical vulnerabilities in changing environments, 3) OPPORTUNITIES: Emerging trends, technological advances, or market shifts that align with organizational capabilities, 4) THREATS: Future risks, industry disruptions, or changing customer

behaviors that could impact business model
viability. Frame each insight with specific
implications for strategic planning and resource
allocation over the next 12-18 months.

Implementation Workflow

Step 1: Document Preparation and Access

1. Compile relevant business documents including strategic plans, market research, financial reports, or competitive analyses
2. Ensure documents contain sufficient detail about business operations, market position, and strategic context
3. Access Microsoft 365 Copilot through Word, Teams, or dedicated Copilot interface
4. Verify document upload capability and formatting compatibility

Step 2: Execute Strategic Analysis Sequence

1. **Initial Assessment:** Apply Master SWOT Analysis prompt to primary strategic document
2. **Competitive Focus:** Use Competitive SWOT prompt if competitive intelligence is available
3. **Future Planning:** Execute Scenario-Based SWOT prompt for forward-looking strategic insights
4. **Synthesis Integration:** Combine insights from multiple analyses into comprehensive strategic assessment

Step 3: Strategic Insight Validation and Enhancement

1. Review generated SWOT analysis for completeness and strategic relevance

2. Cross-reference insights with business knowledge and market understanding
3. Request additional detail on specific strategic factors requiring deeper analysis
4. Integrate quantitative data and specific examples to strengthen strategic recommendations

Step 4: Strategic Communication and Action Planning

1. Structure SWOT insights into executive summary format for stakeholder presentation
2. Prioritize strategic initiatives based on opportunity assessment and capability analysis
3. Develop action plans addressing critical weaknesses and strategic threats
4. Create monitoring framework for tracking strategic factors and competitive positioning

Real-World Strategic Transformation Story

I recall working with a CFO at a European manufacturing firm who initially dismissed strategic analysis as "consultant speak without substance." His company faced declining margins but lacked a systematic approach to strategic assessment. When I demonstrated how Copilot could analyze their annual report and competitive filings to generate comprehensive SWOT analysis, his skepticism transformed into strategic enthusiasm.

Using the Master SWOT Analysis prompt on their 40-page annual report, Copilot identified three critical competitive strengths they had never formally recognized: proprietary manufacturing processes, established distributor relationships, and superior quality certification standards. More importantly, the analysis revealed two strategic threats they had overlooked: emerging low-cost competitors entering their primary markets and changing customer preferences toward sustainable manufacturing practices.

The SWOT analysis became the foundation for their strategic planning retreat, enabling data-driven discussions about resource allocation and competitive positioning. Within six months, they had launched sustainability initiatives leveraging their quality advantages while developing cost reduction strategies to counter competitive threats. The CFO reported that systematic strategic analysis using AI had transformed their planning process from "intuitive guessing to intelligence-driven strategy."

Advanced Strategic Analysis Techniques

Multi-Document Strategic Intelligence Integration: For comprehensive strategic assessment requiring diverse information sources:

```
None
Act as a chief strategy officer conducting
comprehensive organizational analysis using
multiple information sources. I will provide
several business documents including [INSERT
DOCUMENT TYPES: financial reports, market research,
operational assessments, competitive intelligence].
Create an integrated SWOT analysis that synthesizes
insights across all sources, identifying: 1)
STRENGTHS that appear consistently across multiple
data sources, 2) WEAKNESSES that create strategic
vulnerabilities when considered together, 3)
OPPORTUNITIES that emerge from the intersection of
market trends and organizational capabilities, 4)
THREATS that compound across different business
dimensions. Highlight strategic priorities that
address the most critical findings from this
multi-source analysis.
```

Quick Win Testing Protocol

Test 1: Basic SWOT Generation (10 minutes)

1. Select a recent business report, strategic plan, or market analysis document
2. Apply the Master SWOT Analysis prompt to generate comprehensive strategic assessment
3. Verify the analysis identifies relevant internal capabilities and external market factors
4. Compare AI-generated insights with your strategic understanding of the business situation

Test 2: Competitive Strategic Analysis (10 minutes)

1. Use business documentation that includes competitive or market intelligence
2. Execute the Competitive SWOT prompt focusing on market positioning insights
3. Assess whether competitive analysis reveals actionable strategic opportunities
4. Validate competitive threats and positioning insights against market knowledge

Test 3: Cross-Application Strategic Workflow (15 minutes)

1. Apply strategic analysis across multiple document types using different SWOT prompts
2. Synthesize insights from various analyses into coherent strategic narrative
3. Generate executive summary presenting key strategic priorities and recommended actions
4. Measure strategic insight quality improvement compared to manual analysis approaches

These systematic strategic analysis prompts transform Microsoft 365 Copilot into your expert strategy consultant, generating comprehensive SWOT assessments and competitive intelligence without requiring advanced strategic thinking expertise. You now possess the capability to convert any business document into actionable strategic insights, positioning you as the strategic professional who transforms information into competitive advantage while driving evidence-based decision-making through systematic strategic analysis frameworks.

4.2.2 Summarizing Complex Research for Executive Briefings

Executive communication represents the professional skill gap that limits career advancement more than any technical capability. Research indicates that 84% of professionals struggle to distill complex information into executive-appropriate summaries, while 72% report feeling overwhelmed when asked to synthesize multi-source research into actionable recommendations. The average professional spends 3-4 hours manually processing lengthy reports while still delivering summaries that executives find too detailed or lacking strategic insight.

Traditional research synthesis requires advanced analytical skills, strategic thinking expertise, executive communication knowledge, and document synthesis capabilities that most professionals lack. These barriers create systematic communication avoidance that limits strategic contribution while positioning colleagues who master executive briefing as indispensable strategic assets.

Microsoft 365 Copilot transforms research summarization from intimidating bottleneck into systematic executive communication advantage through structured prompts that generate concise, strategic, and action-oriented briefings without requiring advanced synthesis expertise or strategic communication training.

Core Executive Summarization Categories

Effective executive research synthesis requires systematic approaches across five essential communication dimensions:

- **Strategic Executive Summaries:** High-level findings and implications for decision-making
- **Multi-Source Intelligence Integration:** Comprehensive analysis across diverse research documents
- **Action-Oriented Recommendations:** Clear next steps and strategic priorities based on research findings
- **Stakeholder-Specific Briefings:** Customized summaries for different executive audiences and contexts
- **Rapid Research Processing:** Time-efficient workflows for urgent executive communication needs

Category 1: Strategic Executive Summary Generation

Strategic executive summaries convert lengthy research documents into concise, decision-focused briefings that enable rapid executive comprehension and strategic action.

Ready-to-Use Master Executive Summary Prompt:

```
None
Act as a senior management consultant preparing
executive briefings for C-level stakeholders.
Analyze the attached research document and create a
comprehensive executive summary structured as
follows: 1) KEY FINDINGS: 3-4 most critical
discoveries that directly impact business strategy
and operations, 2) STRATEGIC IMPLICATIONS: How
these findings affect competitive position, market
opportunities, and organizational priorities, 3)
RECOMMENDED ACTIONS: 3-5 specific, actionable next
steps with clear ownership and timelines, 4) RISK
ASSESSMENT: Potential consequences of inaction or
delayed response to these findings. Present all
information in executive-appropriate language
focusing on strategic impact rather than tactical
details. Limit total summary to 300-400 words
maximum.
```

Ready-to-Use Three-Bullet Executive Prompt:

> None
>
> Act as an executive strategy advisor creating ultra-concise briefings for time-constrained leadership teams. Review the attached market research report and summarize the key findings, implications, and recommended actions into exactly three bullet points. Each bullet point should: 1) Address a different strategic dimension (market opportunity, competitive threat, operational requirement), 2) Include specific quantitative data where available, 3) Connect findings directly to business impact and required decisions. Format each bullet point as a complete strategic insight that stands alone while contributing to overall strategic narrative. Maximum 75 words per bullet point.

Category 2: Multi-Source Intelligence Integration

Multi-source intelligence integration synthesizes information from diverse research documents into comprehensive strategic assessments that inform complex decision-making.

Ready-to-Use Multi-Document Synthesis Prompt:

> None
>
> Act as a chief strategy officer conducting comprehensive market intelligence analysis using multiple research sources. I will provide several documents including [INSERT DOCUMENT TYPES: market research, competitive analysis, industry reports,

customer surveys]. Create an integrated executive summary that: 1) CONVERGENT FINDINGS: Insights that appear consistently across multiple sources with high confidence levels, 2) CONTRADICTORY INTELLIGENCE: Areas where sources disagree and implications for decision-making uncertainty, 3) STRATEGIC SYNTHESIS: Combined insights that emerge only when considering all sources together, 4) INTELLIGENCE GAPS: Critical information needs that remain unaddressed across all sources. Present findings in priority order based on strategic impact and decision urgency.

Category 3: Action-Oriented Recommendation Development

Action-oriented recommendation development converts research insights into specific, implementable strategic initiatives with clear ownership and success metrics.

Ready-to-Use Strategic Recommendations Prompt:

None
Act as a management consulting partner developing actionable recommendations from research analysis. Based on the attached research findings, generate 5 specific strategic recommendations that follow this structure: 1) RECOMMENDATION: Clear, specific action statement beginning with an action verb, 2) RATIONALE: Brief explanation of research evidence supporting this recommendation, 3) IMPLEMENTATION: Key steps required to execute this recommendation successfully, 4) TIMELINE: Realistic timeframe for implementation and expected results, 5) SUCCESS

```
METRICS: Quantifiable measures to evaluate
recommendation effectiveness. Prioritize
recommendations by potential impact and
implementation feasibility. Focus on actions that
can be initiated within 30-90 days.
```

Category 4: Stakeholder-Specific Executive Briefings

Stakeholder-specific briefings customize research summaries for different executive audiences, ensuring optimal relevance and decision-making support for diverse leadership contexts.

Ready-to-Use CEO-Focused Summary Prompt:

```
None
Act as a senior advisor preparing research
briefings specifically for CEO consumption. Analyze
the attached research and create a CEO-focused
summary addressing: 1) STRATEGIC CONTEXT: How these
findings relate to company vision, market position,
and competitive strategy, 2) CRITICAL DECISIONS:
Specific choices the CEO must make based on this
research with clear trade-offs and implications, 3)
ORGANIZATIONAL IMPACT: Effects on company culture,
resources, and operational priorities, 4)
STAKEHOLDER CONSIDERATIONS: Implications for
investors, board members, customers, and key
partners. Frame all insights in terms of
enterprise-level impact and leadership
requirements. Emphasize long-term strategic
implications over short-term tactical concerns.
```

Ready-to-Use CFO-Focused Summary Prompt:

```
None
Act as a financial strategy consultant creating
research summaries for CFO decision-making. Review
the attached research and develop a CFO-specific
briefing covering: 1) FINANCIAL IMPLICATIONS:
Revenue, cost, and profitability impacts of
research findings with quantified projections where
possible, 2) INVESTMENT REQUIREMENTS: Capital,
operational, and human resource investments needed
to act on research insights, 3) RISK ASSESSMENT:
Financial risks of action versus inaction with
probability estimates, 4) ROI ANALYSIS: Expected
returns and payback timelines for recommended
strategic initiatives. Present all findings with
financial context and business case implications
that support budget planning and resource
allocation decisions.
```

Category 5: Rapid Research Processing Workflows

Rapid research processing enables time-efficient synthesis of urgent research requirements while maintaining executive communication quality and strategic insight depth.

Ready-to-Use Urgent Research Brief Prompt:

```
None
Act as an executive analyst creating time-critical
research briefings for urgent strategic decisions.
Process the attached research document and generate
an immediate-action summary containing: 1) CRITICAL
ALERT: Most important finding requiring immediate
executive attention, 2) DECISION WINDOW: Timeline
```

```
constraints   and   decision   deadlines   based   on
research findings, 3) IMMEDIATE ACTIONS: Steps that
must be taken within 24-48 hours to capitalize on
opportunities  or  mitigate  risks,  4)  INFORMATION
REQUIREMENTS: Additional research or data needed to
support final decision-making. Prioritize speed and
clarity   while   maintaining   strategic   accuracy.
Format  for  immediate  executive  consumption  and
action.
```

Implementation Workflow

Step 1: Research Document Preparation and Analysis

1. Compile all relevant research documents including reports, analyses, studies, and supporting materials
2. Identify primary executive audience and specific decision-making context requiring briefing
3. Determine urgency level and appropriate summary depth based on executive time constraints
4. Access Microsoft 365 Copilot through appropriate application (Word, Teams, or integrated interface)

Step 2: Execute Systematic Summarization Process

1. **Initial Processing:** Apply Master Executive Summary prompt to primary research document
2. **Audience Customization:** Use stakeholder-specific prompts based on intended executive recipient
3. **Multi-Source Integration:** Execute Multi-Document Synthesis prompt when multiple sources require consolidation
4. **Action Development:** Apply Strategic Recommendations prompt to generate implementable next steps

Step 3: Executive Communication Enhancement

1. Review generated summaries for executive-appropriate language and strategic focus
2. Validate quantitative data and specific claims against source material for accuracy
3. Refine recommendations for specificity and implementability within organizational context
4. Structure final briefing for optimal executive consumption and decision-making support

Step 4: Strategic Communication Delivery and Follow-Up

1. Format executive summary for preferred stakeholder communication method (document, presentation, briefing)
2. Prepare supporting materials addressing likely executive questions and concerns
3. Establish follow-up mechanism for tracking strategic decision implementation
4. Create template versions for recurring research summarization requirements

Advanced Research Synthesis Techniques

Comparative Research Analysis: For strategic decision-making requiring multiple research perspective evaluation:

```
None
Act as a strategic intelligence analyst conducting
comparative research evaluation. I will provide
multiple research documents addressing the same
strategic question from different perspectives.
Create a comparative analysis summary that: 1)
METHODOLOGY COMPARISON: Strengths and limitations
of each research approach affecting reliability, 2)
FINDINGS CONVERGENCE: Areas where multiple sources
reach similar conclusions with high confidence, 3)
```

PERSPECTIVE DIFFERENCES: How different research frameworks lead to varying strategic recommendations, 4) SYNTHESIS RECOMMENDATIONS: Integrated strategic guidance that accounts for multiple research perspectives while acknowledging uncertainty areas. Present analysis that enables informed executive decision-making despite research complexity and potential contradictions.

Quick Win Testing Protocol

Test 1: Basic Executive Summary Generation (5 minutes)

1. Select a recent business report, market analysis, or research document exceeding 10 pages
2. Apply the Master Executive Summary prompt to generate comprehensive executive briefing
3. Verify summary captures key strategic insights while remaining within executive attention span
4. Compare AI-generated summary quality with manual summarization approaches

Test 2: Multi-Source Intelligence Integration (10 minutes)

1. Compile 2-3 related research documents addressing similar strategic questions
2. Execute Multi-Document Synthesis prompt to integrate insights across sources
3. Assess whether integrated analysis reveals strategic insights unavailable from individual documents
4. Validate synthesis accuracy and strategic relevance for executive decision-making

Test 3: Stakeholder-Specific Communication (10 minutes)

1. Apply CEO-Focused and CFO-Focused summary prompts to the same research material
2. Compare how audience-specific customization affects strategic emphasis and recommendation focus
3. Evaluate whether customized summaries better serve different executive decision-making needs
4. Test executive receptivity and decision-making support quality of customized briefings

These systematic research summarization prompts transform Microsoft 365 Copilot into your expert executive communication strategist, converting complex research into strategic briefings that enhance decision-making without requiring advanced synthesis expertise. You now possess the capability to distill any research material into executive-appropriate intelligence, positioning you as the strategic professional who bridges analytical complexity and executive clarity while driving informed decision-making through systematic research communication excellence.

5. Integrate Your AI Co-Pilot

You have journeyed through four transformative chapters, systematically building the analytical and operational capabilities that separate AI power users from casual adopters. Your PTCF Framework mastery now spans communication automation, meeting orchestration, and strategic data analysis. Each chapter equipped you with specific prompt categories, systematic approaches, and technical precision that transforms Microsoft 365 Copilot from confusing technology into an indispensable productivity engine.

The foundation you built enables sophisticated single-application workflows: generating complex Excel formulas through natural language, creating executive-level research summaries, automating meeting preparation, and drafting professional communications in seconds rather than hours. You possess technical capabilities that most professionals will never develop, positioning you as the AI-confident colleague who approaches complex challenges with systematic prompt engineering rather than manual effort.

Yet true productivity mastery transcends individual application expertise. The highest-impact professionals orchestrate comprehensive workflows that span multiple applications, connecting discrete tasks into seamless productivity systems that amplify strategic output while minimizing operational overhead. This integration capability separates tactical tool users from strategic productivity leaders who shape organizational efficiency through AI-powered workflow innovation.

The Integration Opportunity

Professional productivity occurs through interconnected processes, not isolated applications. Consider the complexity of launching a strategic initiative: initial concept development, stakeholder research, proposal documentation, presentation creation, team coordination, progress tracking, and executive reporting. Traditional approaches require manual transitions between applications, repetitive data entry, formatting inconsistencies, and coordination overhead that consumes strategic thinking time.

Microsoft 365 Copilot enables systematic workflow integration through cross-application prompt sequences that maintain context, preserve formatting, and eliminate transitional friction. The same PTCF Framework principles that generate precise individual outputs can orchestrate complex multi-stage processes that deliver comprehensive results while requiring minimal manual intervention.

I have observed this integration potential repeatedly across consulting engagements. A director at a multinational consulting firm transformed quarterly planning processes by connecting Excel analysis with Word documentation and PowerPoint presentation creation through systematic prompt sequences. What previously required three weeks of coordination across different team members now completes in two days through integrated AI workflows, enabling faster strategic responses and improved competitive positioning.

The integration opportunity extends beyond time savings to strategic capability enhancement. Connected workflows enable comprehensive analysis that reveals insights unavailable through isolated application use. Cross-referencing data analysis with strategic documentation and presentation development creates layered intelligence that supports superior decision-making and stakeholder communication.

System 1: The End-to-End Workflow Automator

The End-to-End Workflow Automator represents the systematic integration of your accumulated PTCF Framework expertise across multiple applications to complete comprehensive professional processes. This system connects communication automation, analytical processing, strategic synthesis, and presentation development into seamless workflows that deliver complete project outputs.

End-to-end workflow automation requires a systematic approach to prompt sequencing that maintains context consistency while leveraging specialized application capabilities. Each workflow stage employs optimized prompts that build upon previous outputs while preparing inputs for subsequent processing. The result transforms complex multi-day projects into systematic sequences that deliver superior results through AI orchestration.

You will master two complete workflow archetypes that demonstrate integration principles while providing immediate practical value. The Project Kick-Off Workflow guides you through transforming initial concepts into comprehensive action plans including proposal documentation, stakeholder presentations, and team coordination systems. The Monthly Reporting Workflow enables data analysis, strategic synthesis, and executive communication that positions you as the strategic professional who delivers insights rather than just information.

Each workflow archetype employs systematic prompt progression that connects your previously mastered skills: Data Interrogation Engine capabilities feed Strategic Insights Generator processes, which inform Instant Document Drafter outputs, which support Presentation Power-Up development. The integration creates multiplicative rather than additive productivity gains through systematic AI orchestration.

The End-to-End Workflow Automator positions you as the professional who delivers comprehensive solutions rather than tactical outputs. Stakeholders recognize colleagues who consistently produce complete, strategic, and presentation-ready deliverables that advance organizational objectives while demonstrating systematic thinking and execution excellence.

System 2: The Personalized Productivity System

The Personalized Productivity System transforms your accumulated PTCF Framework expertise into customized prompt libraries that address your specific professional context, industry requirements, and recurring workflow needs. This system evolves beyond standardized prompts to create personalized AI interaction protocols that maximize relevance and efficiency for your unique circumstances.

Personalization requires a systematic approach to prompt customization that maintains PTCF Framework structure while optimizing persona specifications, context parameters, and output formats for your professional environment. Generic prompts generate acceptable results, but personalized prompts deliver exceptional outcomes that reflect deep understanding of your industry dynamics, organizational culture, and stakeholder expectations.

You will develop expertise in two critical personalization dimensions that multiply the effectiveness of every prompt you deploy. Role-Specific Customization teaches you to optimize persona and context elements for your job function, industry sector, and organizational level, ensuring AI outputs demonstrate appropriate expertise, terminology, and strategic perspective. Prompt Library Development provides systematic approaches for cataloging, organizing, and refining your highest-performing prompts into accessible repositories that support consistent excellence and continuous improvement.

The personalization process transforms AI interaction from generic tool usage into strategic partnership that understands your professional context and delivers increasingly sophisticated support. Your personalized prompt library becomes intellectual property that enhances your professional capability while creating systematic advantages over colleagues who rely on basic AI interactions.

A senior marketing manager at a technology firm reported that personalizing customer analysis prompts for B2B software contexts improved insight quality by approximately 60% while reducing analysis time by 75%. Her customized prompts incorporated industry-specific metrics, competitive landscape knowledge, and stakeholder communication preferences that generic prompts cannot provide.

The Integration Transformation Promise

This final chapter delivers your evolution from AI tool user to workflow orchestration expert who leverages systematic integration to amplify strategic impact while minimizing operational overhead. You will master end-to-end processes that connect discrete capabilities into comprehensive solutions that position you as an indispensable strategic contributor.

The End-to-End Workflow Automator provides immediate tactical advantages: faster project completion, comprehensive deliverable quality, and systematic approaches to complex professional challenges. You will approach major initiatives with confidence, knowing that AI orchestration enables superior outcomes while reducing time investment and coordination complexity.

The Personalized Productivity System creates long-term strategic advantages: customized AI partnership that understands your professional context, systematic improvement in output quality, and intellectual property development through prompt library creation. Your personalized system evolves continuously, becoming increasingly sophisticated and valuable as you refine and expand your AI interaction capabilities.

Integration mastery distinguishes you as the professional who delivers comprehensive solutions rather than fragmented outputs, strategic insights rather than tactical information, and systematic excellence rather than inconsistent performance. Colleagues, supervisors, and stakeholders recognize individuals who consistently produce complete, strategic, and presentation-ready deliverables that advance organizational objectives.

The transformation extends beyond individual productivity to organizational leadership. Your integration expertise positions you to champion AI adoption within teams, departments, and entire organizations. You become the strategic professional who bridges technology capability and business value, enabling others to realize productivity gains while establishing yourself as workflow innovation leader.

Upon completing this integration chapter, you will possess systematic approaches for orchestrating complex multi-application workflows, personalized prompt libraries that maximize AI partnership effectiveness, and strategic perspective that positions AI as a comprehensive business capability rather than isolated tool functionality. Your professional productivity will operate at levels that seemed impossible before systematic AI integration mastery.

5.1 The End-to-End Workflow Automator

5.1.1 The Project Kick-Off: From Initial Idea to Action Plan

Project initiation represents the comprehensive workflow challenge that separates systematic professionals from reactive task-handlers. Traditional project kick-off processes require weeks of coordination across multiple applications, stakeholders, and documentation formats while maintaining consistency and strategic coherence throughout development stages.

The Project Kick-Off Workflow demonstrates complete PTCF Framework integration across Microsoft 365 applications to transform initial concepts into comprehensive action plans within hours rather than weeks. This end-to-end process connects ideation, documentation, presentation development, and team coordination into seamless AI-orchestrated sequence.

Complete Project Kick-Off Workflow Overview

This comprehensive workflow spans four integrated stages that build upon each other while maintaining contextual consistency:

- **Stage 1:** Concept Development and Strategic Brainstorming
- **Stage 2:** Proposal Documentation and Business Case Creation
- **Stage 3:** Executive Presentation Development and Stakeholder Communication
- **Stage 4:** Team Coordination and Task Distribution Planning

Stage 1: Concept Development and Strategic Brainstorming

Step 1: Initial Concept Generation

1. Open Microsoft Copilot (standalone application or integrated chat interface)
2. Execute comprehensive brainstorming prompt to generate strategic project concepts
3. Review generated ideas for strategic alignment and implementation feasibility
4. Select primary concept for development into full project proposal

Ready-to-Use Strategic Brainstorming Prompt:

```
None
Act as a senior business strategist and innovation
consultant conducting comprehensive project
ideation. I need to develop a strategic initiative
focused on [INSERT PROJECT THEME: digital
transformation/process improvement/market
expansion/product development]. Generate 5 distinct
project concepts that include: 1) PROJECT TITLE:
Memorable, professional name that captures the
initiative's essence, 2) STRATEGIC OBJECTIVE:
Primary business goal and measurable outcome this
project will achieve, 3) KEY ACTIVITIES: 3-4
specific actions required to execute this project
successfully, 4) RESOURCE REQUIREMENTS: High-level
estimation of time, budget, and personnel needs, 5)
SUCCESS METRICS: Quantifiable measures to evaluate
project effectiveness. Structure each concept as a
complete project overview ready for executive
consideration and stakeholder evaluation.
```

Step 2: Concept Refinement and Validation

1. Select the most promising project concept from generated options

2. Apply concept validation prompt to strengthen strategic foundation
3. Document refined concept details for proposal development stage

Ready-to-Use Concept Validation Prompt:

None

Act as a strategic planning expert evaluating project feasibility and business impact. Review this project concept: [PASTE SELECTED CONCEPT]. Strengthen this concept by providing: 1) MARKET OPPORTUNITY: Specific market conditions or business drivers that make this project timely and valuable, 2) COMPETITIVE ADVANTAGE: How this project positions the organization superior to competitors or market alternatives, 3) RISK MITIGATION: Potential challenges and corresponding strategies to ensure project success, 4) STAKEHOLDER VALUE: Specific benefits this project delivers to customers, employees, and organizational leadership, 5) IMPLEMENTATION TIMELINE: Realistic project phases with key milestones and completion targets. Present analysis in executive-appropriate format suitable for business case development.

Stage 2: Proposal Documentation and Business Case Creation

Step 3: Comprehensive Proposal Development

1. Open Microsoft Word and access Copilot integration
2. Execute proposal generation prompt using refined concept details
3. Review generated proposal structure and content for completeness and persuasiveness

Ready-to-Use Project Proposal Generation Prompt:

None

Act as a professional project manager and business writer creating comprehensive project proposals for executive approval. Based on this project concept [PASTE REFINED CONCEPT], draft a complete 3-4 page project proposal with the following structure: 1) EXECUTIVE SUMMARY: Concise overview highlighting project value and recommended approval, 2) PROJECT OVERVIEW: Detailed description of objectives, scope, and expected deliverables, 3) BUSINESS CASE: Financial projections, resource requirements, and return on investment analysis, 4) IMPLEMENTATION PLAN: Project phases, timeline, key milestones, and resource allocation, 5) RISK MANAGEMENT: Potential challenges and mitigation strategies, 6) SUCCESS METRICS: Specific KPIs and measurement criteria for evaluating project effectiveness. Use professional business language appropriate for C-level review and decision-making. Format with clear headings and scannable structure for executive consumption.

Step 4: Proposal Enhancement and Executive Focus

1. Apply proposal refinement prompt to strengthen business case elements
2. Optimize language for executive decision-making and approval processes
3. Finalize proposal document for presentation development stage

Ready-to-Use Proposal Enhancement Prompt:

None

```
Act as an executive communications specialist
optimizing business proposals for C-level approval.
Review this project proposal and enhance: 1)
EXECUTIVE SUMMARY: Strengthen opening paragraph to
immediately communicate value proposition and
recommended action, 2) FINANCIAL JUSTIFICATION:
Improve ROI calculations, cost-benefit analysis,
and budget breakdown for CFO review, 3) STRATEGIC
ALIGNMENT: Better connect project objectives to
organizational priorities and competitive
positioning, 4) IMPLEMENTATION CLARITY: Provide
more specific timeline details and resource
allocation for operational planning, 5) RISK
CONFIDENCE: Strengthen risk mitigation strategies
and contingency planning. Maintain professional
tone while increasing persuasive impact and
decision-making support.
```

Stage 3: Executive Presentation Development and Stakeholder Communication

Step 5: Presentation Structure and Content Creation

1. Open Microsoft PowerPoint and access Copilot integration
2. Execute presentation generation prompt using finalized proposal content
3. Review generated presentation structure for logical flow and executive engagement

Ready-to-Use Presentation Generation Prompt:

None

Act as an executive presentation specialist creating compelling slide presentations for C-level audiences. Using this project proposal [PASTE PROPOSAL CONTENT], create a 8-10 slide PowerPoint presentation with: 1) SLIDE 1: Title slide with project name and presenter information, 2) SLIDE 2: Executive summary highlighting key value proposition and recommendation, 3) SLIDE 3: Project overview and strategic objectives, 4) SLIDE 4: Business case and financial projections, 5) SLIDE 5: Implementation timeline and key milestones, 6) SLIDE 6: Resource requirements and team structure, 7) SLIDE 7: Risk management and mitigation strategies, 8) SLIDE 8: Success metrics and measurement plan, 9) SLIDE 9: Next steps and approval request. Provide clear, concise bullet points for each slide suitable for executive presentation format. Focus on strategic impact rather than tactical details.

Step 6: Speaker Notes and Presentation Delivery Support

1. Generate comprehensive speaker notes for confident presentation delivery
2. Develop anticipated questions and strategic responses for stakeholder Q&A sessions

Ready-to-Use Speaker Notes Generation Prompt:

None

Act as an executive presentation coach developing speaker notes for confident project proposal delivery. For this presentation outline [PASTE

PRESENTATION STRUCTURE], create detailed speaker notes for each slide including: 1) KEY TALKING POINTS: 3-4 specific points to emphasize during each slide presentation, 2) SUPPORTING DETAILS: Additional context and examples to strengthen key arguments, 3) TRANSITION PHRASES: Smooth connections between slides that maintain audience engagement, 4) ANTICIPATED QUESTIONS: Likely stakeholder inquiries and strategic responses that reinforce project value, 5) CLOSING REINFORCEMENT: Compelling summary statements that drive toward approval decision. Structure notes for easy reference during live presentation while maintaining professional confidence and strategic authority.
```

## Stage 4: Team Coordination and Task Distribution Planning

### Step 7: Comprehensive Task Planning and Team Organization

1. Open Microsoft Teams and access Copilot integration
2. Execute task planning prompt to create systematic project coordination
3. Generate team communication templates for consistent project execution

### Ready-to-Use Project Task Planning Prompt:

```
None
Act as a senior project manager creating comprehensive task management plans for successful project execution. Based on this approved project proposal [PASTE PROPOSAL SUMMARY], develop detailed

task breakdown including: 1) PROJECT PHASES: Distinct stages with clear objectives and completion criteria, 2) TASK INVENTORY: Specific activities required for each phase with estimated effort and dependencies, 3) TEAM ASSIGNMENTS: Role-based task distribution with clear ownership and accountability, 4) TIMELINE COORDINATION: Sequence planning that optimizes resource utilization and minimizes scheduling conflicts, 5) MILESTONE TRACKING: Key checkpoints with deliverable specifications and success criteria, 6) COMMUNICATION PROTOCOLS: Regular check-in schedules, reporting requirements, and stakeholder update procedures. Format as actionable project plan suitable for immediate team implementation and progress monitoring.

Step 8: Team Communication and Coordination Setup

1. Generate team announcement templates for project kick-off communication
2. Create recurring meeting agenda templates for consistent progress tracking
3. Establish project documentation and collaboration protocols

Ready-to-Use Team Coordination Prompt:

None

Act as a project leadership specialist creating team communication materials for successful project launch. Develop comprehensive team coordination package including: 1) PROJECT ANNOUNCEMENT:

```
Professional team communication introducing project
objectives, timeline, and individual roles, 2)
KICK-OFF MEETING AGENDA: Structured first meeting
agenda covering project overview, role
clarification, and initial task assignments, 3)
WEEKLY CHECK-IN TEMPLATE: Recurring meeting
structure for progress updates, obstacle
resolution, and coordination planning, 4) STATUS
REPORTING FORMAT: Standardized progress
communication template for consistent stakeholder
updates, 5) COLLABORATION GUIDELINES: Clear
protocols for document sharing, decision-making
authority, and issue escalation procedures. Format
materials for immediate implementation and
sustainable project management excellence.
```

Integration Workflow Execution Summary

This complete Project Kick-Off Workflow demonstrates PTCF Framework mastery across integrated Microsoft 365 applications while delivering comprehensive project initiation in systematic sequence. Each stage builds contextual consistency while leveraging specialized application capabilities for optimal results.

The workflow transforms weeks of traditional project development into focused AI-orchestrated process that delivers superior strategic thinking, documentation quality, and team coordination efficiency. Your integrated approach positions you as the strategic professional who approaches complex initiatives with systematic excellence while minimizing coordination overhead and maximizing stakeholder value.

5.1.2 THE MONTHLY REPORT: FROM RAW DATA TO FINAL PRESENTATION

Monthly performance reporting represents the recurring workflow challenge that consumes disproportionate time while delivering inconsistent strategic value. Traditional monthly reporting requires hours of manual data analysis, document formatting, presentation development, and coordination across multiple stakeholders, often resulting in delayed insights that limit decision-making effectiveness.

The Monthly Report Workflow demonstrates complete PTCF Framework integration to transform raw performance data into executive-ready presentations within 30-45 minutes rather than 6-8 hours. This systematic approach ensures consistent analysis depth, professional presentation quality, and strategic insight delivery that positions you as an indispensable business intelligence asset.

Complete Monthly Report Workflow Overview

This comprehensive three-stage workflow maintains contextual consistency while leveraging specialized application capabilities:

- **Stage 1:** Data Analysis and Trend Identification using Excel Copilot
- **Stage 2:** Strategic Summary Documentation using Word Copilot
- **Stage 3:** Executive Presentation Development using PowerPoint Copilot

Stage 1: Data Analysis and Trend Identification

Step 1: Raw Data Processing and Initial Analysis

1. Open Microsoft Excel with your monthly performance dataset

2. Access Excel Copilot through ribbon interface or chat integration
3. Execute comprehensive data analysis prompt to identify performance patterns
4. Review generated insights for accuracy and strategic relevance

Ready-to-Use Monthly Performance Analysis Prompt:

```
Act as a senior business analyst conducting
comprehensive monthly performance evaluation.
Analyze this dataset and provide detailed insights
including: 1) TOP PERFORMERS: Identify the 5
highest performing metrics, products, or categories
with specific values and percentage changes from
previous month, 2) CONCERNING TRENDS: Highlight 3-4
metrics showing decline or underperformance with
quantified impact, 3) MONTH-OVER-MONTH COMPARISONS:
Calculate percentage changes for all key metrics
compared to previous month, 4) NOTABLE PATTERNS:
Identify seasonal trends, unusual spikes, or
systematic changes requiring attention, 5) KEY
OPPORTUNITIES: Areas showing improvement potential
based on data trends. Present analysis in executive
summary format with specific numbers and actionable
insights for strategic decision-making.
```

Step 2: Competitive and Contextual Analysis

1. Apply advanced analysis prompt to understand performance within broader business context
2. Generate specific recommendations based on data patterns and trend analysis
3. Document key findings for integration into summary document stage

Ready-to-Use Strategic Context Analysis Prompt:

```
None
Act as a strategic business consultant providing
context for monthly performance data. Based on this
analysis [PASTE PREVIOUS ANALYSIS], provide
strategic insights including: 1) BUSINESS IMPACT
ASSESSMENT: How these performance trends affect
overall organizational objectives and competitive
position, 2) ROOT CAUSE ANALYSIS: Potential
explanations for significant changes in key
metrics, considering market conditions and
operational factors, 3) STRATEGIC IMPLICATIONS:
What these trends suggest about future performance
and required business adjustments, 4) PRIORITY
RECOMMENDATIONS: 3-5 specific actions to capitalize
on positive trends and address concerning patterns,
5) RISK FACTORS: Potential challenges or threats
indicated by current performance data. Structure
insights for executive consumption and strategic
planning applications.
```

Stage 2: Strategic Summary Documentation

Step 3: Executive Summary Document Creation

1. Open Microsoft Word and access Copilot integration
2. Execute comprehensive summary generation prompt using Excel analysis results
3. Review document structure and content for executive communication standards

Ready-to-Use Monthly Report Summary Prompt:

None

```
Act as an executive communications specialist
creating monthly performance reports for C-level
review. Using this performance analysis [PASTE
EXCEL ANALYSIS RESULTS], draft a comprehensive 2-3
page monthly report with following structure: 1)
EXECUTIVE SUMMARY: Concise overview highlighting
key performance achievements and concerns requiring
immediate attention, 2) PERFORMANCE HIGHLIGHTS:
Major accomplishments and positive trends with
supporting data and metrics, 3) AREAS OF CONCERN:
Underperforming metrics with analysis of potential
causes and recommended corrective actions, 4)
STRATEGIC INSIGHTS: Broader implications of
performance trends for business strategy and
competitive positioning, 5) RECOMMENDED ACTIONS:
Specific next steps with ownership assignments and
timeline expectations, 6) OUTLOOK: Forward-looking
assessment of expected performance trends and
strategic priorities. Use professional business
language appropriate for executive decision-making
while maintaining clarity and actionability.
```

Step 4: Document Enhancement and Quality Assurance

1. Apply document refinement prompt to optimize language and strategic focus
2. Ensure consistency between data analysis and narrative summary
3. Finalize document for presentation development stage

Ready-to-Use Report Enhancement Prompt:

None

Act as a senior business editor optimizing executive reports for maximum impact and clarity. Review this monthly performance report and enhance: 1) EXECUTIVE LANGUAGE: Strengthen opening paragraphs to immediately communicate key insights and recommended decisions, 2) DATA INTEGRATION: Improve connection between specific metrics and strategic conclusions, ensuring all claims are supported by concrete evidence, 3) ACTIONABILITY: Make recommendations more specific and implementable with clear ownership and timelines, 4) STRATEGIC FOCUS: Enhance strategic context and business implications while maintaining executive-appropriate brevity, 5) PRESENTATION READINESS: Structure content to support seamless translation into presentation format. Maintain professional tone while increasing persuasive impact and decision-making support.

Stage 3: Executive Presentation Development

Step 5: Presentation Structure and Slide Development

1. Open Microsoft PowerPoint and access Copilot integration
2. Execute presentation generation prompt using finalized report content
3. Review slide structure for logical flow and executive engagement

Ready-to-Use Monthly Report Presentation Prompt:

None

Act as an executive presentation specialist creating compelling monthly performance presentations for senior leadership teams. Using this monthly report [PASTE REPORT CONTENT], create a 8-12 slide presentation with: 1) SLIDE 1: Title slide with reporting period and presenter information, 2) SLIDE 2: Executive summary highlighting month's key achievements and priority concerns, 3) SLIDE 3: Performance dashboard showing critical metrics with visual indicators, 4) SLIDE 4: Top performing areas with supporting data and success factors, 5) SLIDE 5: Areas requiring attention with impact analysis and proposed solutions, 6) SLIDE 6: Month-over-month trend analysis with contextual insights, 7) SLIDE 7: Strategic implications and business impact assessment, 8) SLIDE 8: Recommended actions with ownership and timeline specifications, 9) SLIDE 9: Forward-looking outlook and strategic priorities, 10) SLIDE 10: Questions and discussion facilitation. Provide clear, concise bullet points optimized for executive presentation delivery and strategic discussion.

Step 6: Visual Enhancement and Delivery Preparation

1. Generate speaker notes and presentation delivery support materials
2. Create anticipated questions and strategic responses for stakeholder engagement
3. Finalize presentation for executive delivery

Ready-to-Use Presentation Delivery Support Prompt:

None

```
Act as an executive presentation coach developing
comprehensive   delivery   support   for   monthly
performance presentations. For this presentation
outline [PASTE PRESENTATION STRUCTURE], create: 1)
DETAILED SPEAKER NOTES: Key talking points for each
slide with supporting context and examples that
reinforce data insights, 2) SMOOTH TRANSITIONS:
Professional connections between slides that
maintain audience engagement and logical flow, 3)
ANTICIPATED QUESTIONS: Likely stakeholder inquiries
about performance data, trends, and recommendations
with strategic responses that demonstrate thorough
analysis,   4)   VISUAL   ENHANCEMENT   SUGGESTIONS:
Recommendations for charts, graphs, or visual
elements that strengthen data communication and
executive comprehension, 5) CLOSING REINFORCEMENT:
Compelling summary statements that drive toward
strategic decision-making and action commitment.
Structure   materials   for   confident   executive
presentation delivery and productive strategic
discussion.
```

Integration Workflow Execution Protocol

Complete Workflow Timeline:

- **Minutes 1-15:** Excel data analysis and trend identification using systematic prompts
- **Minutes 16-30:** Word document creation and strategic summary development
- **Minutes 31-45:** PowerPoint presentation generation and delivery preparation

Quality Assurance Checkpoints:

1. **Data Accuracy Validation:** Cross-reference AI-generated insights with source data for mathematical precision
2. **Narrative Consistency:** Ensure alignment between Excel analysis, Word summary, and PowerPoint presentation
3. **Executive Communication Standards:** Verify language, formatting, and strategic focus meet C-level expectations
4. **Actionability Assessment:** Confirm all recommendations include specific ownership and timeline commitments

Advanced Integration Techniques

Cross-Application Context Maintenance:

```
None
Act as a workflow integration specialist ensuring
consistency across Microsoft 365 applications.
Review this content progression: Excel Analysis →
Word Summary → PowerPoint Presentation. Identify
and resolve any inconsistencies in data
presentation, strategic messaging, or
recommendation specificity. Ensure seamless
narrative flow that maintains executive confidence
and supports strategic decision-making across all
deliverable formats.
```

This comprehensive Monthly Report Workflow transforms traditional reporting challenges into a systematic AI-orchestrated process that delivers consistent strategic value while minimizing time investment. Your integrated approach positions you as the strategic professional who converts raw performance data into actionable business intelligence that drives organizational decision-making and competitive advantage through systematic excellence and presentation quality.

5.2 THE PERSONALIZED PRODUCTIVITY SYSTEM

5.2.1 CUSTOMIZING PROMPTS FOR YOUR SPECIFIC ROLE AND INDUSTRY

Generic prompts generate acceptable results, but personalized prompts deliver exceptional outcomes that reflect deep understanding of your professional environment. The difference between universal and customized AI interaction determines whether Copilot functions as a basic assistant or strategic partner who understands your industry dynamics, organizational culture, and stakeholder expectations.

Prompt personalization requires systematic modification of PTCF Framework elements to optimize relevance and effectiveness for your unique professional context. This customization process transforms standard prompts into precision instruments that generate outputs demonstrating appropriate expertise, terminology, and strategic perspective for your specific role and industry sector.

PTCF Framework Personalization Overview

Effective prompt customization focuses on two critical framework elements that drive contextual relevance:

- **Persona Customization:** Modifying the "Act as" component to reflect your specific job function, expertise level, and professional responsibilities
- **Context Customization:** Adapting situational parameters to include industry-specific requirements, organizational standards, and stakeholder expectations

Step 1: Role and Industry Assessment

1. **Identify Your Primary Professional Function**

- Document your official job title and primary responsibilities
- List the top 3-5 tasks that consume most of your professional time
- Note specific expertise areas that differentiate your role from similar positions
- Identify key stakeholders who consume your work outputs

2. **Assess Your Industry Context**

    - Define your industry sector using standard classifications (technology, healthcare, finance, manufacturing, etc.)
    - List industry-specific terminology and metrics commonly used in your field
    - Identify regulatory requirements or compliance standards affecting your work
    - Note competitive dynamics and market conditions influencing your industry

3. **Document Organizational Standards**

    - Review your company's communication style and formatting preferences
    - Identify decision-making hierarchies and approval processes
    - Note data security requirements and confidentiality protocols
    - List internal tools, systems, and methodologies used in your organization

Step 2: Persona Element Customization

Basic Persona Customization Process:

1. Start with generic "Act as a [ROLE]" format
2. Add specific expertise qualifiers that enhance credibility
3. Include industry context that shapes perspective

4. Specify experience level appropriate for your responsibilities

Ready-to-Use Persona Templates by Function:

Financial Professionals:

```
Act as a senior financial analyst with 8+ years of
experience in corporate finance and investment
analysis, specializing in [INSERT SPECIFIC AREA:
mergers and acquisitions/budget planning/risk
assessment/financial modeling]
```

Marketing Professionals:

```
Act as an experienced marketing manager with
expertise in digital marketing and brand strategy,
focusing on [INSERT SPECIFIC AREA: B2B lead
generation/content marketing/campaign
optimization/market research]
```

Operations Professionals:

```
Act as a seasoned operations manager with extensive
experience in process optimization and team
leadership, specializing in [INSERT SPECIFIC AREA:
supply chain management/quality assurance/project
delivery/efficiency improvement]
```

Technology Professionals:

```
None
Act as a senior technology professional with deep
expertise in enterprise systems and digital
transformation, focusing on [INSERT SPECIFIC AREA:
software                        development/data
analysis/cybersecurity/infrastructure management]
```

Human Resources Professionals:

```
None
Act as an experienced HR business partner with
comprehensive knowledge of talent management and
organizational development, specializing in [INSERT
SPECIFIC    AREA:      recruitment/performance
management/employee relations/compliance]
```

Step 3: Context Element Customization

Industry-Specific Context Enhancement:

1. Replace generic business references with industry-appropriate terminology
2. Include regulatory or compliance requirements relevant to your sector
3. Reference industry-standard metrics and performance indicators
4. Incorporate competitive landscape considerations specific to your market

Healthcare Industry Context Example:

None

Operating within healthcare regulatory environment requiring HIPAA compliance, focus on patient safety outcomes and evidence-based practices while considering healthcare economics and quality improvement initiatives

Financial Services Context Example:

None

Working within financial services regulatory framework including SEC compliance and fiduciary responsibilities, emphasizing risk management, regulatory adherence, and stakeholder value creation

Technology Sector Context Example:

None

Operating in fast-paced technology environment prioritizing innovation, scalability, and competitive positioning while managing technical debt and user experience optimization

Manufacturing Industry Context Example:

None

Functioning within manufacturing operations emphasizing safety protocols, quality standards, operational efficiency, and supply chain resilience while managing cost controls and productivity targets

Step 4: Practical Customization Examples

Base Task: Analyze quarterly performance data and create executive summary

Generic Prompt:

None
Act as a business analyst and review this quarterly performance data. Create an executive summary highlighting key trends and recommendations.

Customized for Financial Analyst:

None
Act as a senior financial analyst with expertise in corporate finance and investment analysis. Review this quarterly performance data focusing on revenue recognition, margin analysis, and cash flow implications. Create an executive summary for CFO review that highlights financial trends, identifies variance explanations, and provides recommendations for optimizing financial performance while ensuring regulatory compliance and stakeholder value creation.

Customized for Marketing Manager:

None

Act as an experienced marketing manager with expertise in digital marketing and brand strategy. Review this quarterly performance data focusing on customer acquisition costs, lifetime value metrics, and channel performance. Create an executive summary for CMO review that highlights marketing effectiveness trends, identifies optimization opportunities, and provides recommendations for improving campaign ROI and market share growth.

Customized for Operations Manager:

None

Act as a seasoned operations manager with extensive experience in process optimization and efficiency improvement. Review this quarterly performance data focusing on operational metrics, productivity indicators, and quality measurements. Create an executive summary for COO review that highlights operational performance trends, identifies process bottlenecks, and provides recommendations for enhancing efficiency while maintaining safety standards and cost controls.

Step 5: Advanced Customization Techniques

Stakeholder-Specific Customization:

1. Modify persona to reflect your relationship with specific stakeholders
2. Adjust formality level based on organizational hierarchy

3. Include decision-making authority considerations
4. Reference specific business units or functional areas

Executive Communication Customization:

```
None
Act as a senior [YOUR ROLE] preparing materials for
C-level executive review. Focus on strategic
implications rather than tactical details,
emphasize business impact and competitive
positioning, and structure recommendations for
rapid decision-making by time-constrained
leadership.
```

Peer Collaboration Customization:

```
None
Act as a collaborative [YOUR ROLE] working with
cross-functional teams. Emphasize practical
implementation considerations, acknowledge diverse
perspectives, and structure information for
effective team coordination and project execution.
```

Client Communication Customization:

```
None
Act as a client-facing [YOUR ROLE] representing
your organization's expertise and value
proposition. Maintain professional authority while
demonstrating understanding of client objectives,
emphasize outcomes and benefits, and structure
```

communication for maximum client confidence and engagement.

Step 6: Testing and Refinement Process

1. **Initial Customization Implementation**

    - Apply your customized persona and context to existing prompts
    - Test customized prompts on familiar tasks to assess improvement quality
    - Compare outputs between generic and customized prompt versions
    - Document specific improvements in relevance and usefulness

2. **Iterative Enhancement Protocol**

    - Identify areas where outputs still lack industry specificity
    - Refine persona descriptions to better reflect your expertise level
    - Adjust context parameters based on stakeholder feedback
    - Test refined prompts on increasingly complex tasks

3. **Quality Validation Checklist**

    - Does the output demonstrate appropriate industry knowledge?
    - Are terminology and metrics relevant to your professional environment?
    - Would stakeholders recognize this as coming from someone with your expertise?
    - Are recommendations practical within your organizational constraints?

This systematic customization approach transforms your PTCF Framework prompts into precision instruments that generate outputs reflecting deep understanding of your professional context, industry dynamics, and stakeholder expectations, positioning you as the AI-confident professional who leverages personalized prompting for maximum strategic advantage.

5.2.2 Building a Personal Library of High-Performance Prompts

Prompt library development transforms occasional AI success into systematic productivity advantage. Without organized prompt management, even the most effective prompts become forgotten experiments that cannot be replicated or refined. Professional excellence requires systematic capture, organization, and continuous improvement of your highest-performing PTCF Framework prompts.

Your personal prompt library serves as intellectual property that appreciates in value through systematic refinement and expansion. This library becomes your competitive advantage, enabling consistent high-quality outputs while reducing the time investment required for complex tasks. The difference between professionals who achieve AI mastery and those who struggle lies in systematic prompt library development.

Step 1: Select Your Prompt Library Platform

Platform Option 1: Microsoft OneNote (Recommended)

1. Open Microsoft OneNote and create new notebook titled "AI Prompt Library"
2. Create separate sections for each major workflow category:
   - Email and Communication Prompts
   - Document Creation Prompts
   - Meeting and Collaboration Prompts

- Data Analysis and Insights Prompts
- Cross-Application Workflow Prompts
3. Within each section, create pages for specific prompt categories
4. Use OneNote's search functionality to quickly locate prompts by keyword or task type

Platform Option 2: Microsoft Word Document System

1. Create master document titled "Personal Copilot Prompt Library"
2. Use heading styles to create navigable table of contents
3. Organize prompts using consistent formatting with heading hierarchy
4. Save document in easily accessible location with regular backup protocol
5. Use Word's navigation pane for quick prompt location and retrieval

Platform Option 3: Microsoft Excel Spreadsheet Database

1. Create Excel workbook with separate worksheets for each prompt category
2. Use columns for: Prompt Name, PTCF Components, Full Prompt Text, Use Case, Performance Rating, Last Updated
3. Apply filters and sorting capabilities for advanced prompt organization
4. Use conditional formatting to highlight highest-performing prompts

Step 2: Implement Systematic Prompt Capture Protocol

Immediate Capture Process:

1. **Test and Validate:** Before adding any prompt to your library, test it at least twice on different tasks to confirm consistent quality

2. **Document Context:** Record the specific situation where the prompt performed exceptionally well
3. **Rate Performance:** Use 5-point scale to evaluate prompt effectiveness and output quality
4. **Note Customizations:** Document any modifications made to base prompts for your specific needs

Prompt Documentation Template:

```
None
PROMPT NAME: [Descriptive title for easy identification]

CATEGORY: [Primary workflow category]

PTCF BREAKDOWN:

- Persona: [Specific role/expertise designation]

- Task: [Exact action requested]

- Context: [Situational parameters and constraints]

- Format: [Output structure and presentation requirements]


FULL PROMPT TEXT:

[Complete, copy-pasteable prompt ready for immediate use]


USE CASES:

• [Specific situation 1]

• [Specific situation 2]
```

- [Specific situation 3]

```
PERFORMANCE NOTES:

- Effectiveness Rating: [1-5 scale]

- Best Results When: [Optimal conditions for this prompt]

- Avoid Using When: [Situations where prompt underperforms]

- Last Updated: [Date of most recent modification]
```

Step 3: Organize Prompts by Strategic Value

Tier 1: Daily Essential Prompts Prompts you use multiple times per week that deliver consistent high-value results:

- Email summarization and response generation
- Meeting preparation and follow-up automation
- Document drafting and editing for routine communications
- Quick data analysis and trend identification

Tier 2: Weekly Power Prompts Complex prompts for recurring but less frequent high-impact tasks:

- Comprehensive report generation workflows
- Strategic analysis and business case development
- Cross-application project management sequences
- Stakeholder communication and presentation creation

Tier 3: Specialized Expertise Prompts Industry-specific or role-specific prompts for specialized professional requirements:

- Regulatory compliance documentation
- Technical analysis and problem-solving
- Creative content development and marketing materials
- Financial modeling and budget planning

Step 4: Establish Prompt Refinement Workflow

Monthly Prompt Audit Process:

1. **Performance Review:** Evaluate which prompts delivered exceptional results during the month
2. **Usage Analysis:** Identify frequently used prompts that could benefit from optimization
3. **Gap Assessment:** Note missing prompts for recurring tasks currently handled manually
4. **Refinement Priority:** Select 3-5 prompts for improvement based on usage frequency and potential impact

Prompt Improvement Protocol:

1. **Analyze Suboptimal Outputs:** Document specific areas where current prompts fall short of expectations
2. **Research Enhancement Options:** Test variations in persona specification, context parameters, or format requirements
3. **A/B Test Modifications:** Compare original prompt performance with enhanced versions on similar tasks
4. **Document Improvements:** Update library with refined prompts and performance comparison notes
5. **Archive Previous Versions:** Maintain version history for prompts that undergo significant modifications

Step 5: Create Prompt Combination Strategies

Sequential Prompt Chaining: Document workflows where multiple prompts work together to complete complex tasks:

```
None
WORKFLOW NAME: Quarterly Business Review
Preparation

STEP 1 PROMPT: [Data analysis and trend
identification]

STEP 2 PROMPT: [Strategic insights generation and
synthesis]

STEP 3 PROMPT: [Executive summary document
creation]

STEP 4 PROMPT: [Presentation outline and slide
development]

STEP 5 PROMPT: [Speaker notes and delivery
preparation]


TOTAL TIME INVESTMENT: [Estimated completion time]

EXPECTED OUTCOMES: [Specific deliverables and
quality standards]
```

Cross-Application Integration Sequences: Capture systematic approaches that leverage multiple Microsoft 365 applications:

- Excel analysis feeding Word documentation feeding PowerPoint presentations
- Teams meeting transcripts informing Outlook communication strategies
- Word document content optimized for specific stakeholder presentations

Step 6: Implement Sharing and Collaboration Protocols

Team Prompt Sharing Guidelines:

1. **Confidentiality Assessment:** Ensure prompts contain no sensitive organizational information before sharing
2. **Standardization Process:** Adapt personal prompts for broader team use by removing role-specific elements
3. **Training Documentation:** Create usage guides for shared prompts including optimization tips and common pitfalls
4. **Feedback Collection:** Establish mechanism for team members to suggest improvements and report effectiveness

Prompt Library Backup and Security:

1. **Regular Backup Schedule:** Export prompt library monthly to secure location
2. **Version Control:** Maintain dated backups to enable recovery of previous prompt versions
3. **Access Management:** Ensure prompt library remains accessible across devices and platforms
4. **Security Considerations:** Protect prompts containing organizational methodologies or competitive advantages

Step 7: Measure and Optimize Library Impact

Performance Tracking Metrics:

- **Time Savings:** Document hours saved per week through systematic prompt library usage
- **Quality Improvements:** Track stakeholder feedback and output quality enhancements
- **Task Completion Rate:** Monitor increased ability to handle complex projects efficiently
- **Professional Recognition:** Note career advancement opportunities enabled by AI-enhanced productivity

Continuous Improvement Indicators:

1. **Prompt Usage Frequency:** Identify most valuable prompts requiring further refinement
2. **Output Consistency:** Assess reliability of prompt performance across different contexts
3. **Adaptation Success:** Evaluate effectiveness of customized prompts for new situations
4. **Knowledge Transfer:** Measure success in sharing effective prompts with colleagues

Your personal prompt library represents intellectual property that compounds in value through systematic development and refinement. This organized approach to prompt management transforms Microsoft 365 Copilot from a helpful tool into an indispensable strategic asset that elevates your professional capabilities while establishing you as the AI-confident expert who approaches complex challenges with systematic precision and consistent excellence.

Conclusion

You have completed a remarkable transformation. When you first opened this book, you faced the same productivity challenges that plague millions of professionals: email overwhelm, meeting inefficiency, document creation bottlenecks, and the persistent feeling that technology worked against you rather than for you. You possessed the same Microsoft 365 applications that everyone else used, but you lacked the strategic framework to unlock their true potential through AI partnership.

That person no longer exists.

You now possess systematic mastery of the PTCF Framework, a proprietary methodology that transforms Microsoft 365 Copilot from helpful assistant into strategic productivity engine. This transformation extends far beyond learning new software features. You have fundamentally rewired how you approach professional challenges, moving from reactive task completion to proactive workflow orchestration.

The professional who struggled with basic prompt creation has evolved into someone who crafts precise, strategic AI commands that deliver consistent, high-quality results. You no longer guess what might work or rely on trial and error. Instead, you apply systematic principles that ensure every interaction with Copilot advances your strategic objectives while maintaining professional standards.

Your relationship with technology has shifted from user to director. You now understand that artificial intelligence augments human intelligence most effectively when guided by clear, structured communication. The PTCF Framework provides that structure, enabling you to delegate repetitive tasks with confidence while reserving your cognitive capacity for creativity, critical thinking, and strategic innovation.

Your Comprehensive Skill Arsenal

Foundational Mastery:

- **Co-Pilot Mindset:** You understand AI as augmentation partner, not replacement technology, positioning you to leverage emerging capabilities while maintaining strategic control
- **PTCF Framework Fluency:** You construct prompts using Persona, Task, Context, and Format elements that deliver precise, professional outputs consistently
- **Iterative Refinement Expertise:** You optimize prompt performance through systematic analysis and adjustment, ensuring continuous improvement in output quality

Communication Excellence:

- **Zero-Inbox System Mastery:** You process email threads instantly through strategic summarization and generate professional responses in seconds rather than minutes
- **Instant Document Creation:** You defeat blank page syndrome through systematic first-draft generation and refine content for any audience with precision editing prompts
- **Professional Communication Optimization:** You adapt tone, formality, and complexity for specific stakeholders while maintaining consistent quality standards

Meeting and Collaboration Leadership:

- **Automated Meeting Management:** You prepare comprehensive briefings, generate strategic agendas, and extract actionable insights from meeting transcripts with systematic efficiency

- **Presentation Development Mastery:** You transform documents into compelling presentations and create speaker notes that enhance delivery confidence and audience engagement
- **Collaborative Workflow Orchestration:** You coordinate team communication and project management through AI-enhanced productivity systems

Analytical and Strategic Capabilities:

- **Data Interrogation Expertise:** You generate complex Excel formulas through natural language commands and identify trends and outliers without manual analysis
- **Strategic Insights Generation:** You create comprehensive SWOT analyses from business documents and synthesize complex research into executive-ready summaries
- **Evidence-Based Decision Making:** You transform raw information into actionable intelligence that supports strategic planning and competitive positioning

Integration and Personalization Mastery:

- **End-to-End Workflow Automation:** You orchestrate complex multi-application processes from initial concept through final deliverable with systematic precision
- **Role-Specific Customization:** You adapt generic prompts for your industry, function, and organizational context, maximizing relevance and effectiveness
- **Personal Productivity System Development:** You build and maintain prompt libraries that capture your highest-performing AI interactions for systematic reuse and continuous improvement

Your Competitive Advantages

Your PTCF Framework mastery creates multiple layers of professional advantage that compound over time. You complete complex projects in substantially less time while maintaining superior quality standards. This efficiency gain enables you to take on additional strategic responsibilities or invest saved time in skill development and relationship building.

Your systematic approach to AI interaction produces consistent, predictable results that stakeholders recognize and value. Colleagues notice your ability to generate comprehensive analysis, professional documentation, and strategic insights with remarkable speed and accuracy. This reliability positions you as the professional who delivers excellence under pressure while maintaining calm, systematic execution.

Your understanding of AI augmentation principles prepares you for emerging technologies and capabilities. As Microsoft 365 Copilot evolves and new AI tools emerge, you possess the foundational knowledge to adapt quickly and maintain your competitive edge. Your prompt engineering expertise translates across platforms and applications, making you technology-agnostic in your productivity excellence.

Your Strategic Next Steps

Phase 1: Systematic Implementation and Optimization (Next 30 Days)

Your immediate priority involves cementing the PTCF Framework as your default approach to AI interaction. Focus on implementing your most valuable prompts across daily workflows while building systematic habits that reinforce long-term success.

Daily Practice Protocol:

- Use PTCF Framework prompts for all Copilot interactions, avoiding the temptation to revert to casual, unstructured requests
- Document successful prompts in your personal library immediately after achieving exceptional results

- Rate prompt performance using your 5-point effectiveness scale to identify optimization opportunities
- Test prompt variations systematically rather than making random changes

Weekly Optimization Review:

- Analyze which prompts delivered the highest value during the week and prioritize their refinement
- Identify workflow gaps where new prompts could eliminate manual processes
- Share successful approaches with colleagues to establish yourself as AI productivity expert
- Update prompt documentation with performance insights and usage notes

Monthly Strategic Assessment:

- Calculate time savings achieved through systematic AI integration across all workflow categories
- Evaluate professional recognition and career advancement opportunities enabled by enhanced productivity
- Assess prompt library growth and identify missing capabilities that require development
- Plan advanced skill development in emerging AI applications and methodologies

Phase 2: Leadership and Knowledge Transfer (Days 31-90)

Your next development phase focuses on establishing yourself as an organizational AI productivity leader while expanding your influence through knowledge sharing and team development.

Internal Leadership Initiatives:

- Volunteer to lead AI productivity training sessions for colleagues and team members

- Create standardized prompt templates for common organizational tasks and workflows
- Develop best practices documentation that enables systematic AI adoption across departments
- Mentor other professionals in PTCF Framework implementation and optimization

Cross-Functional Collaboration:

- Partner with IT departments to integrate AI productivity training into organizational development programs
- Collaborate with project managers to embed AI-enhanced workflows into standard operating procedures
- Work with training teams to develop comprehensive AI productivity certification programs
- Contribute to organizational AI governance and ethical usage policy development

External Recognition Building:

- Share AI productivity insights through professional networking platforms and industry forums
- Speak at conferences or webinars about practical AI implementation in professional environments
- Write articles or blog posts detailing specific use cases and success stories from your experience
- Build reputation as thought leader in practical AI application for business productivity

Phase 3: Innovation and Future Readiness (Days 91+)

Your long-term development strategy positions you at the forefront of AI-enhanced productivity while building capabilities that translate across emerging technologies and platforms.

Advanced Capability Development:

- Explore integration opportunities between Microsoft 365 Copilot and other AI platforms for comprehensive workflow automation
- Develop expertise in prompt engineering for specialized industry applications and use cases
- Master advanced analytical techniques that leverage AI for strategic business intelligence and competitive analysis
- Build proficiency with emerging AI tools and platforms that complement your Microsoft 365 expertise

Strategic Business Impact:

- Lead organizational initiatives that demonstrate measurable ROI from AI productivity implementation
- Develop business cases for expanded AI tool adoption based on documented performance improvements
- Create systematic approaches for measuring and reporting AI productivity impact across organizational levels
- Establish yourself as strategic advisor for AI-driven business process optimization and competitive advantage

Continuous Learning and Adaptation:

- Maintain cutting-edge knowledge of AI productivity developments through systematic research and experimentation
- Build relationships with AI productivity experts and thought leaders to access emerging best practices
- Participate in beta programs and early access initiatives for new AI productivity tools and features
- Contribute to the broader AI productivity community through knowledge sharing and collaborative development

Your Future Impact and Potential

The PTCF Framework mastery you have achieved represents the foundation of a fundamental shift in how professional work gets accomplished. You are positioned at the leading edge of a transformation that will define competitive advantage for the next decade and beyond.

Your systematic approach to AI augmentation creates exponential rather than linear productivity gains. As you refine your prompt library and expand your capabilities, your efficiency improvements compound while your strategic impact multiplies. The time you save through AI-enhanced task completion enables deeper focus on high-value activities that drive career advancement and professional recognition.

Your expertise positions you to shape organizational AI adoption strategies and influence industry best practices. Companies need professionals who can bridge the gap between AI potential and practical implementation. Your combination of technical proficiency and strategic understanding makes you invaluable for organizations navigating AI transformation.

The professional landscape is rapidly dividing between those who master AI augmentation and those who struggle with traditional approaches to productivity challenges. Your PTCF Framework expertise places you firmly in the first category, creating sustainable competitive advantages that strengthen over time.

You began this journey seeking solutions to common productivity frustrations. You have emerged with systematic mastery of revolutionary technology that transforms how professional work gets accomplished. Your PTCF Framework expertise represents intellectual property that appreciates in value through application and refinement.

More importantly, you have developed the mindset and capabilities needed to thrive in an AI-augmented professional environment. Your understanding of systematic prompt engineering, strategic AI partnership, and continuous optimization positions you for sustained success regardless of how specific technologies evolve.

The productivity system you have mastered enables you to reclaim time for what matters most: strategic thinking, creative problem-solving, meaningful relationship building, and impactful contribution to organizational success. You are no longer constrained by administrative overhead or repetitive task completion. Instead, you direct your energy toward high-value activities that advance your career and amplify your professional impact.

Your productivity revolution starts now.

Acknowledgements

I want to thank the remarkable people who made this book possible.

First, to my mentor, the former Silicon Valley COO who taught me that the most successful technology is not the most powerful, but the most human-centric. Your wisdom shaped my entire approach to AI productivity and continues to guide my work every day.

To my early clients who trusted me with their workflows and became willing test subjects for these prompt engineering methods. Your feedback, patience, and willingness to experiment helped refine every technique in this book. You proved that these systems work in the real world.

To my family and friends who supported me through countless late nights of writing and research. You listened to my excitement about prompt frameworks with genuine interest and reminded me to take breaks when I needed them most.

Finally, to every professional who feels overwhelmed by technology rather than empowered by it. This book exists because I believe you deserve better tools and clearer guidance for reclaiming your time.

Savannah Johnson

www.ingramcontent.com/pod-product-compliance
Lightning Source LLC
Chambersburg PA
CBHW052144220526
45471CB00004B/1524